WILLIAM SCOTT

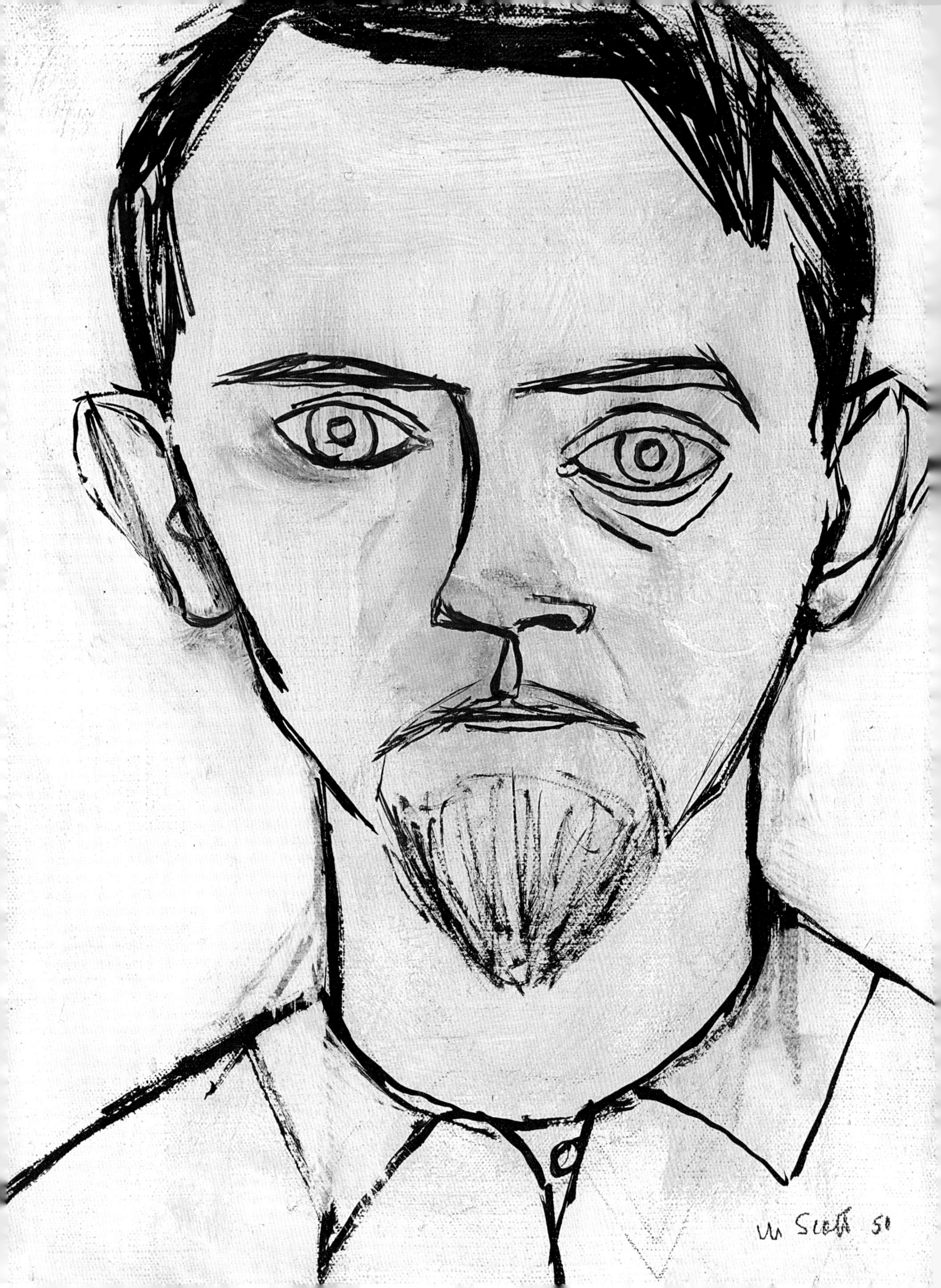
W Scott 51

WILLIAM SCOTT

BRITISH ARTISTS

SARAH WHITFIELD

TATE PUBLISHING

First published 2013 by order of the Tate Trustees
by Tate Publishing, a division of Tate Enterprises Ltd,
Millbank, London SW1P 4RG
www.tate.org.uk/publishing

A catalogue record for this book is available from the British Library.
ISBN 978 1 84976 082 9

Distributed in the United States and Canada by Harry N. Abrams, Inc., New York
Library of Congress control number: 2012947082

Designed by Webb & Webb

Colour reproduction by DL Imaging Ltd, London

Printed in Hong Kong by Great Wall Printing Company Ltd

Front cover: William Scott, *Harbour* 1952 (see fig.16)
Frontispiece: William Scott, *Self Portrait* 1950, Oil on canvas,
28 x 22, Tate Archive

Measurements of artworks are given in centimetres, height before width.

CONTENTS

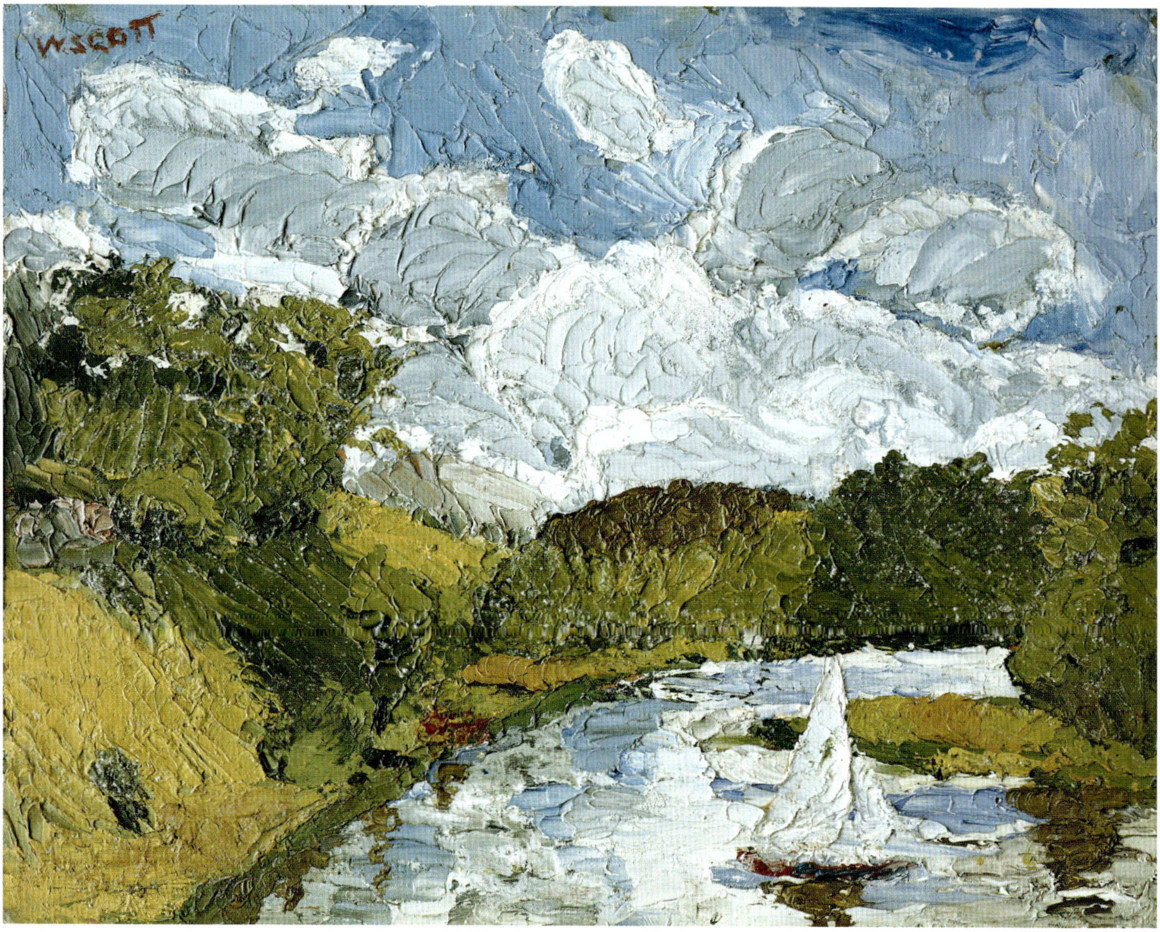

1

Lough Erne, Enniskillen

1928

Oil on board

27.6 x 35.7

Private collection

1 A GREY WORLD

A GUIDEBOOK to William Scott's hometown of Enniskillen in County Fermanagh published in 1912, the year before Scott was born, described the town as 'one of the prettiest places in Ireland'. Surrounded by the river that unites the upper and lower parts of Lough Erne, it had from almost every point of view, the guidebook promised, 'a particularly beautiful appearance'.[1] Scott's earliest known painting (fig.1), a small canvas dated 1928, when he was fifteen years old, echoes the brightness of that description. Indeed, the scene of breezy white clouds above the ruffled blue of the lough might have been borrowed from a cheerful picture postcard.

In later life Scott remembered that landscape rather differently, claiming that the constantly changing greys he saw in the skies of Fermanagh provided his first lessons in tonal painting. He was not born in Enniskillen but in Greenock, the Scottish port built on a long narrow stretch of the River Clyde. His parents lived in a small flat at the top of one of the tall granite tenements near the quay, and it was there that he spent his early childhood. He never forgot the grim aspect of those impoverished surroundings. 'There were a lot of bridges, tunnels, stations and steps', he remembered, 'stone bridges that you went over and iron bridges you went under – bits of ground between streets that had never been built on growing nettles, and in the summer littered with small pieces of dirty paper.'[2] His parents, William and Agnes Scott, and their seven children lived in three rooms with beds built into the walls. A lavatory on the landing was shared with two other flats, while twelve families had the use of a single wash house at the back of the building. Agnes Scott was Scottish by birth, but her husband came from Enniskillen and had often talked of taking his family back to settle in Ulster, a move energetically resisted by Agnes. In 1924, however, when the young William was eleven years old, his father, without a word to his family, caught the boat to Londonderry, and on his arrival in Enniskillen wrote his wife a brief letter instructing her to sell everything and join him. Life in Northern Ireland was not much easier than in Greenock, but the surroundings were less brutal. While Greenock was a noisy port polluted by the nauseating mixture of smells from the gasworks, the bone works and the sugar refineries, Enniskillen was a small country town surrounded by the peaceful waters of Lough Erne. And instead of the squalor of the overpopulated tenements, the houses in Enniskillen were whitewashed, small and built at ground floor level, with stable doors 'good for leaning out in summer weather'.

The iron-dark greys of Greenock, the softer greys of Fermanagh, and the pale scuffed whites of the small Northern Irish houses are colours that recur frequently in Scott's painting, a reminder of the tenacious grip landscape can have on a painter's memory. There was another reason why Scott remembered his childhood as shadowed. In November 1927 his father was killed in his attempt to rescue a person from a blazing building. A fire had broken out in a shop on the main street that runs through Enniskillen, and Scott's father, who was passing by, volunteered to carry a hose up an extension ladder. The ladder snapped in two and he was flung onto the paved street.

Father and son had been close: William senior had earned his living as a sign painter and decorator, a trade he had begun to pass on to his son, teaching him the rudiments of glazing, gilding and lettering but all the time thinking ahead to a better future. 'He was a humble house painter', Scott recalled, 'but he wanted me to be an artist. I'm sure he didn't know what an artist was but he knew it was on a higher level.'[3] Whatever ideas William John Scott may have had, he knew enough to persuade a young art teacher, recently arrived in Enniskillen, to take his son under her wing. Kathleen Bridle allowed the young boy to attend her afternoon classes and two evening classes at the Enniskillen Technical School as a special pupil, free of charge. Bridle was a young painter just out of the Royal College of Art in London, with a very good knowledge of modern painting, which she had every intention of sharing with her young students. Her collection of art books, as well as her teaching, was Scott's introduction to a world he had no other way of knowing. She remembered him as 'a very eager little boy who worked and worked', and who was so keen that 'he used to come to my flat and root among my books and draw with me when I went out at weekends'.[4] Scott tried to help his widowed mother financially by painting small landscapes he could sell locally. *Lough Erne, Enniskillen* is the only evidence that has been traced of these youthful efforts to supplement the family income. It was also thanks to Bridle's friendship with the local art inspector that the county council granted Scott a scholarship (with funds put together from the local community) to attend the Belfast School of Art.

Before he set foot in the Belfast Art Gallery for the first time in 1928, the only art he knew at first hand were Bridle's watercolours and portraits commissioned by local patrons, and the paintings his father liked to copy from old postcards of Greenock. In Belfast, however, he was able to see recent works by Augustus John, William Orpen and, most memorably, Stanley Spencer, whose large religious painting *The Betrayal* was acquired by the gallery in 1929. Scott may have had little experience of looking at art, but thanks to Bridle's library he had a mind stocked with images of works by modern masters such as Paul Cézanne and André Derain, painters whom the teachers at Belfast School of Art refused even to discuss with their students. Their silence, as Scott was quick to appreciate, came as much from ignorance as disapproval. The first two years at the school were spent drawing from the antique, and from life. To begin with, Scott was not allowed to see the naked female model, who was hidden from the younger students by a screen illuminated from behind to show her in silhouette (making outline studies of the nude was an exercise that Scott never forgot: the nudes he drew and painted in his later years capture something of the innocence of that early experience).

Although Scott always spoke warmly about Northern Ireland and later returned to Enniskillen many times, as a young man he could not wait to leave. The opportunity came when he learned that the Royal Academy Schools in London offered free tuition. Calculating that he stood a better chance of getting into the Sculpture School than the Painting School, he applied and was accepted. In late September 1931, he and a fellow student from Belfast, William Tocher, left for England. As Scott boarded the boat, he saw an evening newspaper with a headline announcing the death of Orpen, an Irish artist who made his career in London. Turning to his friend, he asked him if he had seen the announcement, to which Tocher replied that he had, adding 'that leaves a place for you'.

Scott had not distinguished himself at Belfast (he appears to have failed his final exams). The Royal Academy Schools was a grander institution but also strictly academic and permeated by a similar atmosphere of antiquity. Like many students arriving in London for the first time, Scott had acquired an exaggerated idea of the great metropolis (he cannot have been alone in finding Piccadilly Circus only half the size he expected). Although his drawing teacher Walter Thomas 'Tom' Monnington is said to have found Scott a rebellious student, the school records show that he worked hard, and made a point of winning prizes. These came with cash rewards, a huge incentive for an impoverished student from Ulster trying to survive in times of general hardship. And Scott found the going very tough. He took odd jobs such as painting postcards for a printing firm (which went bust), doing domestic work, and at one point working on the totalisator board at the Stamford Bridge greyhound track. Hard as it was, the economic depression of the early 1930s affected Scott less than some of his contemporaries because, as he said himself, he had always lived in a society of the socially depressed. He made many friends, indeed one of his fellow students reported that he knew no one else in London with as many friends as Scott, 'yet he is a sight or would be to anyone who didn't know him as we do. He's so frail looking, one eye looks a wee bit off where you'd expect it to be when he looks at you as a result of being hit with a stone when young.'[5] A suit he wore for a whole year was so caked in clay and plaster it became unrecognisable.

In 1934 Scott transferred at his own request from the Sculpture School to the Painting School. While he told the authorities that he had discovered that his inclination lay 'in the direction of painting', he later maintained that the change had been for practical reasons: 'One had to be pretty mobile in the early thirties. We changed our digs so frequently that the less gear we had to drag from one place to another the better. Besides, landladies were more tolerant to painters. They were rather against their bedrooms being used as a sculptor's studio.'[6] Whether Scott's decision to change course was made from conviction or convenience, the move paid off

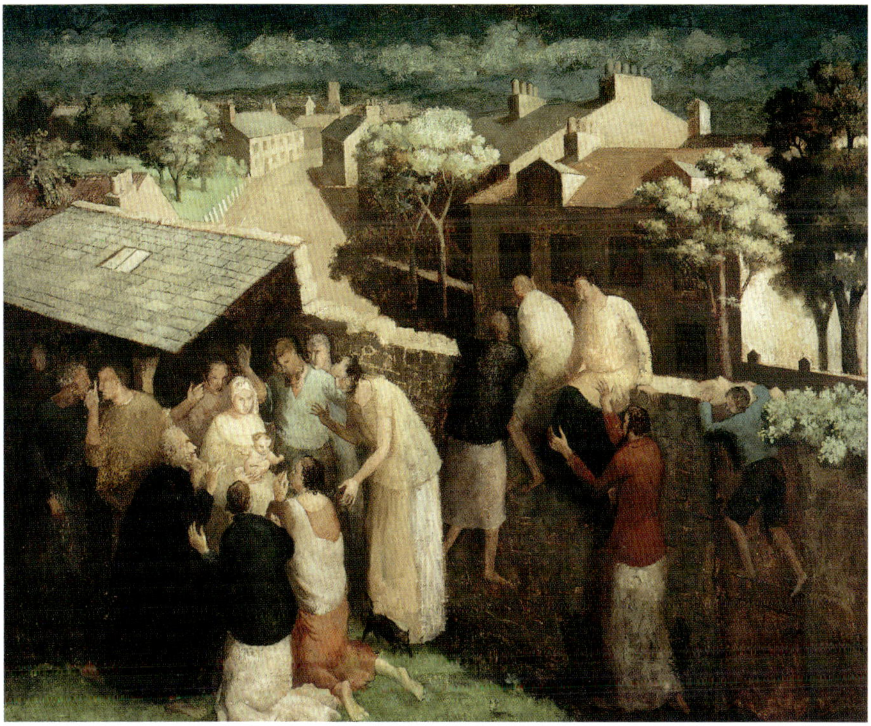

2
The Adoration of the Shepherds
1935
Oil on canvas
102.3 x 127.2
Private collection

when in July he was awarded a Landseer painting scholarship of £40 a year for two years. The ambition of every painting student was to win the Gold Medal, a prize that came with £200, a sum particularly tempting to Scott, whose grant from Northern Ireland had come to an end. The subject that year was *The Adoration of the Shepherds* (fig.2).

Looking back on this period, Scott described his generation of art students as 'victims of the aesthetic dilemma of the thirties', a dilemma he saw as the gulf between the leading movements such as surrealism and post-cubist abstraction, art that he found too remote from the economic realities of 'three million unemployed, hunger marches from the North and industrial chaos in Wales'. His conclusion that, 'the period of group thinking was over and each of us had to search for something that might fit the time or suit ourselves' was probably the most important idea he took away from his student days. What suited Scott at this particular moment was the example of Stanley Spencer, whose contemporary settings of Christian imagery encouraged him to depict *The Adoration of the Shepherds* against the background of a Bethlehem transformed into a Northern Irish village. The painting failed to win him the Gold Medal, however. It was, declared

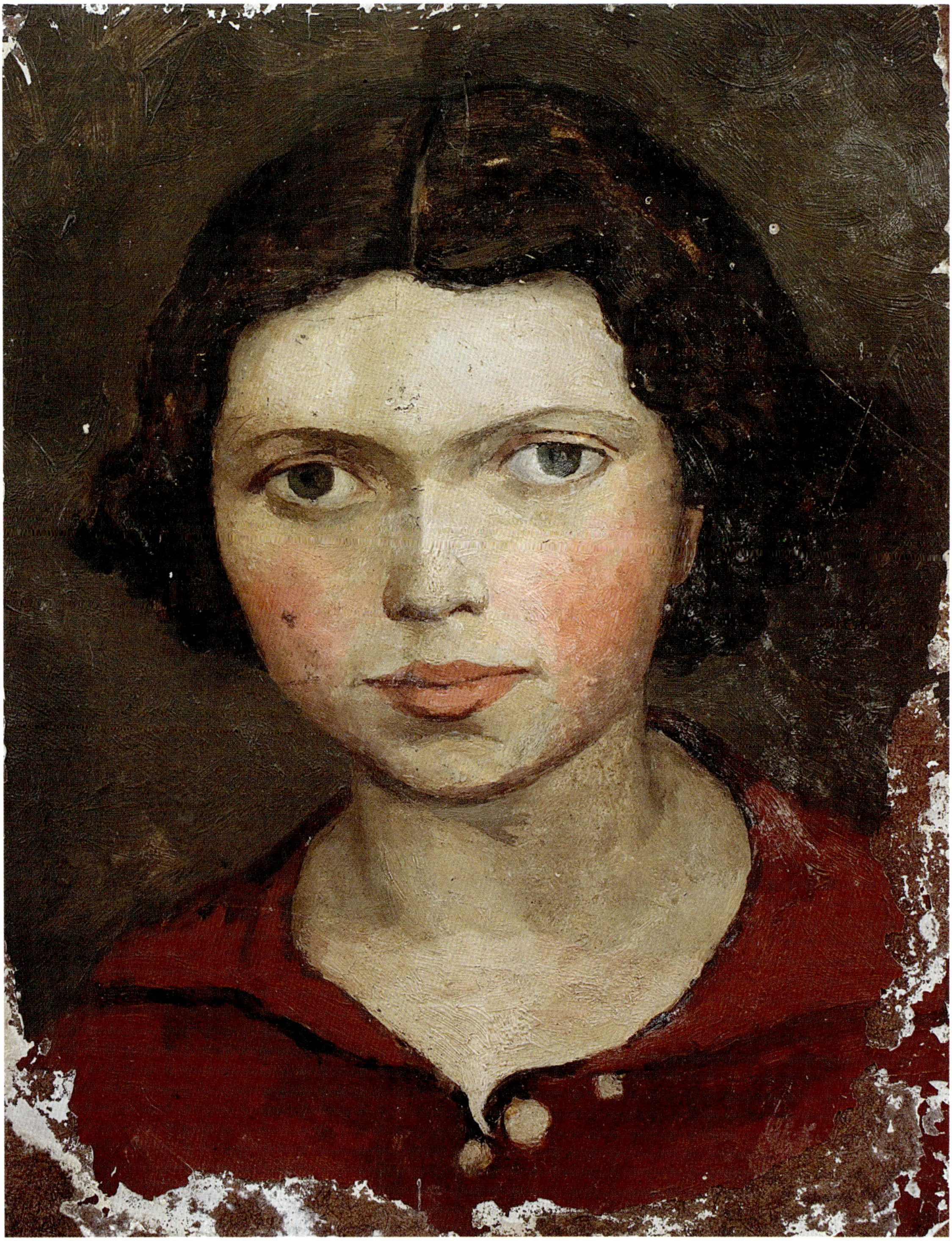

one of his art-school friends, 'a Sinn Fein sort of a painting', a remark that showed a grasp of Scott's intentions if not his Presbyterian background.

Spencer was Scott's introduction to a vein in English painting he himself described as 'primitive realism'. In September 1935, before he had officially left the Royal Academy, he moved to Mousehole, a small Cornish fishing village, where he stayed in a fisherman's loft that had been converted into a small studio. There he met Laura and Harold Knight, both Royal Academicians, as well as the painter Dod Procter. Scott described this change of scene as his 'first break'. 'I had seen the work of Christopher Wood in London and I saw Cornwall through his eyes. I was also acquainted with the paintings of Alfred Wallis, and I started to think of primitive realism as something to be aimed for.' The names he associated with this type of realism, Henri Rousseau, Amedeo Modigliani, Pierre Bonnard and Henri Matisse, were all painters he claimed had more meaning for him than 'the whimsy of Paul Klee which was making a strong appeal to the literary world at that time',[7] a remark that may have reflected the opinion of his friend the Welsh poet Dylan Thomas, who, so it is said, had a hand in painting the tiles on the manger roof of the *Adoration*. Although Scott was never closely associated with the artistic colony at St Ives in the way that contemporaries of his such as Patrick Heron and Peter Lanyon came to be, he made regular visits to that part of Cornwall right up to the late 1950s. The Irish painter T.P. Flanagan, who, like Scott, came from County Fermanagh, once said of him that 'the lessons of landscape were always just at the corner of his eye'. If only a few paintings taken directly from nature can be attributed to Scott, he was nevertheless acutely aware of his landscape surroundings. When looking for somewhere to settle, he sought out parts of England or France that were largely untouched by modern cultivation (like the dozens of islands that can be found on Lough Erne), or unspoiled land whose contours retained a sense of prehistory (like the rugged coasts of Cornwall and Brittany).

In May 1937 Scott married Hilda Mary Lucas (fig.3), a sculpture student at the Royal Academy Schools who had arrived there just as Scott transferred to the Painting School. Mary Lucas, as she was known, had done well at the Royal Academy, winning prizes, as well as a Landseer scholarship. Together with Scott's own scholarship money and an allowance from Mary's father, who owned a paint manufacturing business outside Bristol (Colthurst and Harding Ltd), they had enough money to get

3
Portrait of Mary
1934
Oil on board
29.2 x 23.3
Private collection

married and to think of moving to France or Italy, where the cost of living was cheaper. On 30 December 1937, the Scotts left England, settling first in Alassio on the Ligurian Riviera, from where they could visit Florence, and where for the first time Scott was able to look at early Italian Renaissance painters such as Giotto. But the couple soon moved on. Following a visit to Pont-Aven in Brittany and a chance meeting with a former Slade student called Geoffrey Nelson, the three young artists decided to stay in the area and set up a summer art school. Scott had a knack of making useful contacts, and it may have been through Nelson that he met the French painter Maurice Asselin, a friend of Walter Richard Sickert (who had taught Nelson), and well known enough in Paris to be able to recommend young painters to his friends on the jury of the Salon d'Automne in Paris. This he did for Scott, who was duly invited to show in the British section of the 1938 Salon d'Automne, an unexpected piece of luck for a completely unknown twenty-five year old. It was the start of a regular pattern. Scott, who had learned earlier than most that he had to depend on himself to get anywhere as a painter, rarely let a chance to exhibit slip by. Between the three of them, the Scotts and Nelson drummed up an impressive list of supporters for the 'Pont-Aven School of Painting', including Augustus John, Sir Muirhead Bone and Sickert. The timing could not have been worse. The school opened in May, and on 3 September war with Germany was declared. On 29 August, the Scotts left France in a hurry, catching a boat from Saint Malo. Nelson refused to leave Pont-Aven and was taken prisoner by the Germans. He did not survive the war.

During the two years Scott spent away from England, he concentrated on the figure, often using Mary as his model. The nudes he painted in Pont-Aven are usually half clothed (fig.4), and although his tonal range of colour owes much to his admiration for the portraits by the nineteenth-century French painter Camille Corot, the forms of the figure have a solidity that are consistent with both the sculpture he had produced at the Royal Academy a few years earlier and the figures by Giotto he had recently seen in Florence and Padua. Dedication to tonal painting on the one hand and to solid sculptural form on the other are typical of Scott's work, and help explain why landscape although 'always at the corner of his eye' remained a subject implied rather than tackled directly. In works such as *Breton Church* (fig.5) and *Breton Landscape* (fig.6), both painted in 1938, it is the buildings that hold the painter's attention: the solidity of the three triangular blocks in *Breton Church* is emphasised by the light striking and flattening the walls

4
Seated Nude
1939
Oil on canvas
50.8 x 40.6
Tate. Presented by Mr and Mrs Eugene Rosenberg through the Friends of the Tate Gallery 1968

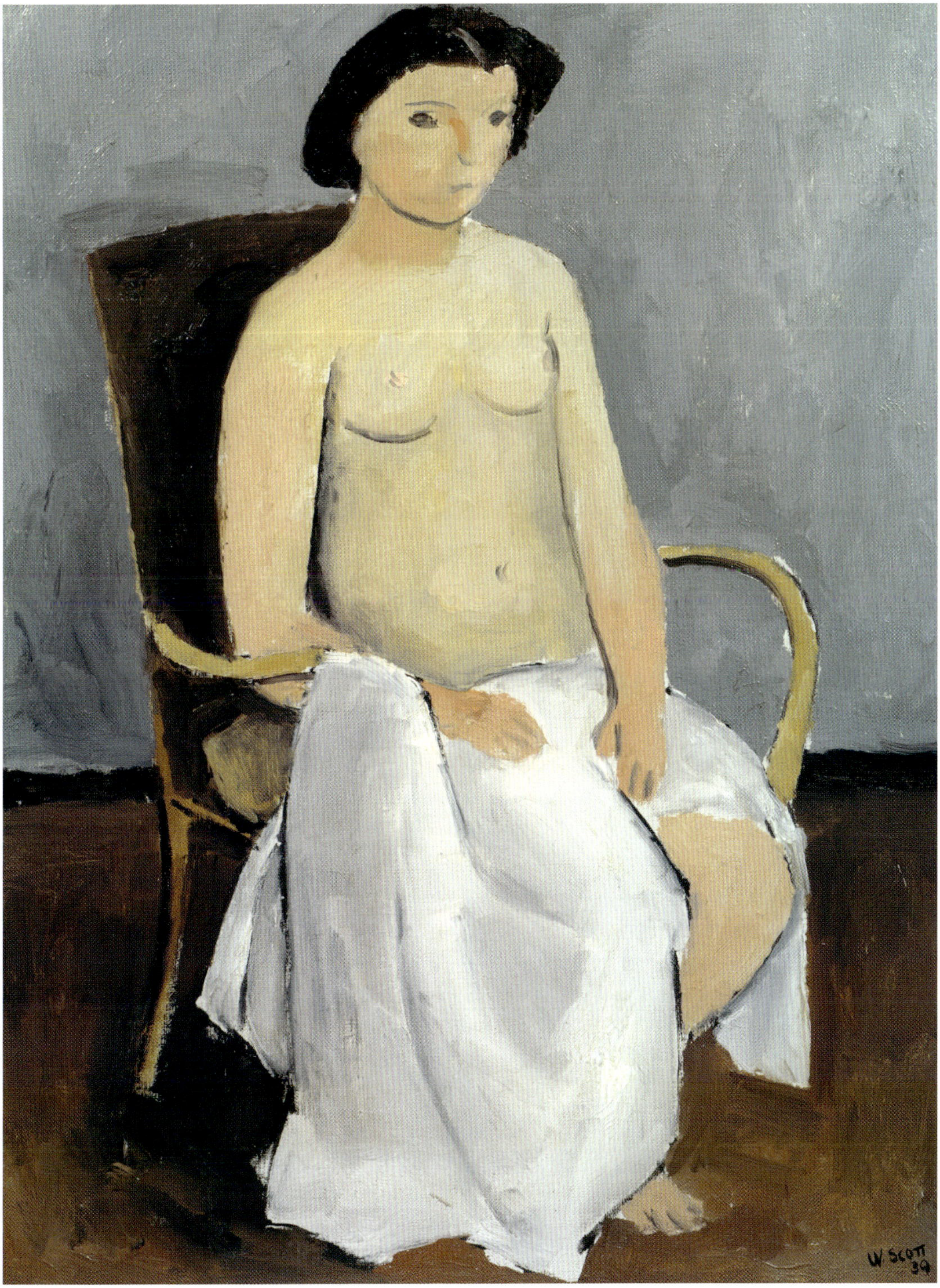

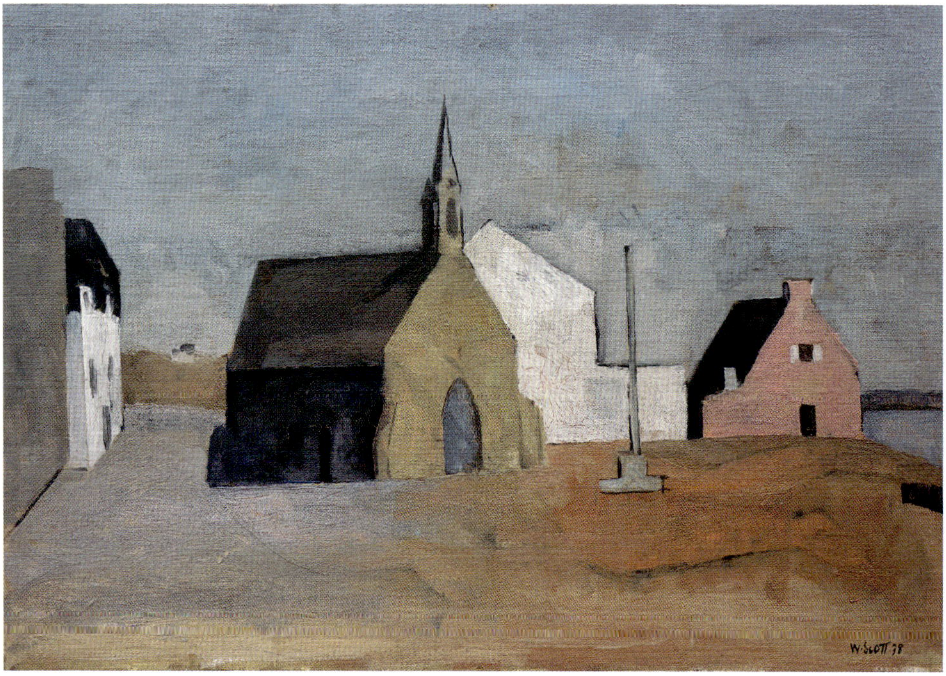

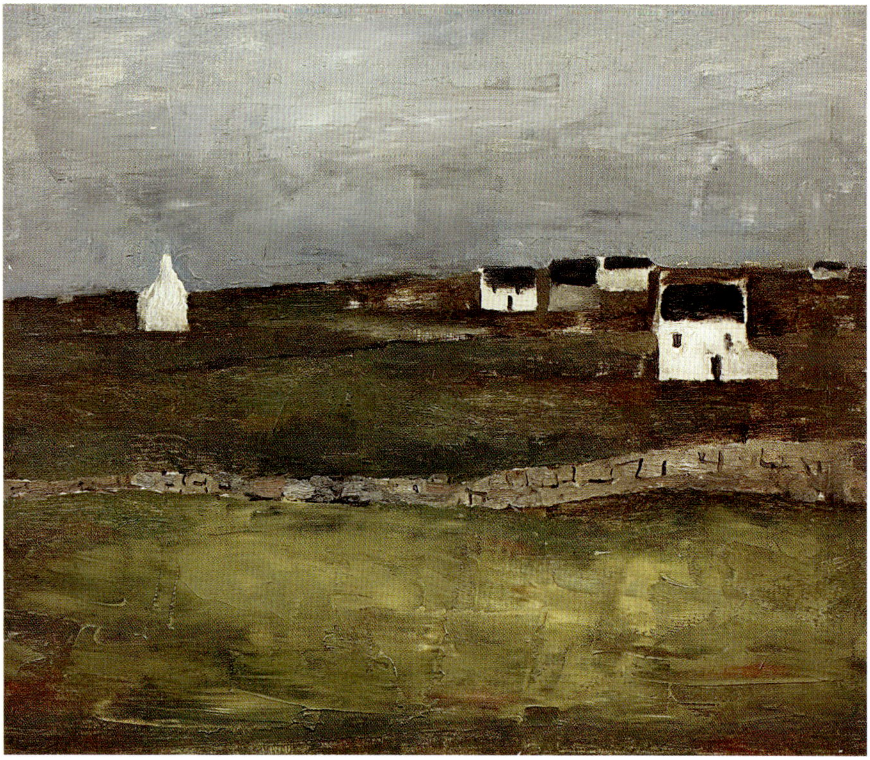

5

Breton Church

1938

Oil on board

44.5 x 64.8

Private collection

6

Breton Landscape

1938

Oil on canvas

32 x 39.6

Private collection

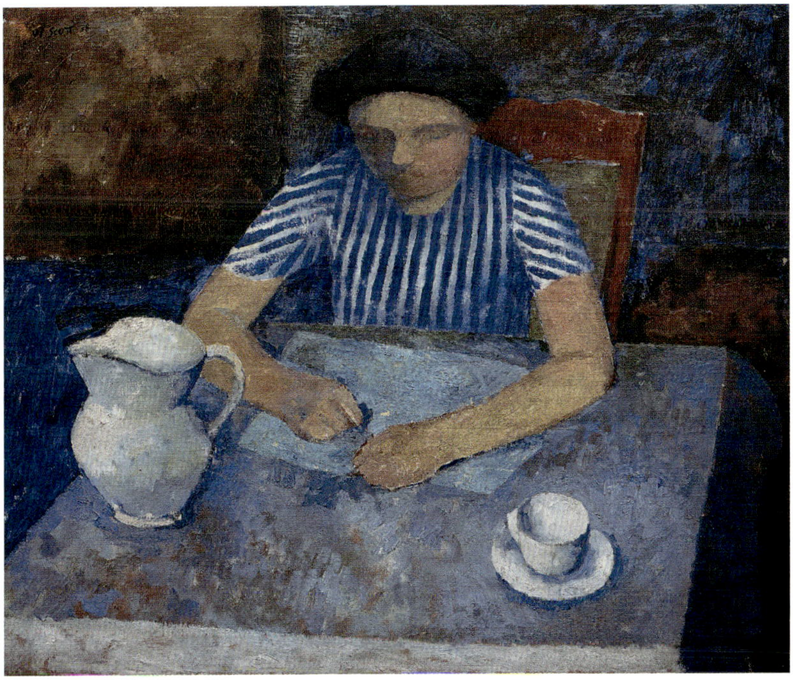

7
Girl and Blue Table
1938
Oil on canvas
65.9 x 81
Leicestershire County Council

(painted in typical Corot-like pinks and greys), while in *Breton Landscape* the empty green of the fields are relieved by houses that look like little white boxes with black lids. In the foreground, a stone wall runs along the ground, an early example of Scott's lifelong affection for these ancient boundaries. (A friend of his recalls being asked to stop the car in some town they happened to be passing through so that Scott could climb out and run his hand over an old wall).[8] His affinity with the man-made rather than with nature is seen in two other works painted in Pont-Aven, *Girl and Blue Table* (fig.7) and *Flowers with Red Drapery* (fig.8). The girl seated at the blue table is recognisably Mary Scott. Her face is carved and her nose chiselled flat in the manner of a Cycladic figurine: she is as solid an object as the white china jug and teacup and saucer placed at either side of the table. And even when Scott turns his attention to fabric and flowers, which he does in *Flowers with Red Drapery*, it is the substantial piece of white Breton pottery that holds everything in place rather than the unstable jumble of textiles. (The subject is easier to read once it is understood that the checked cloth and the white tasseled cotton belong to a half-glimpsed bed.)

In these four paintings – *Breton Church*, *Breton Landscape*, *Girl and Blue Table* and *Flowers with Red Drapery* – Scott declares his admiration

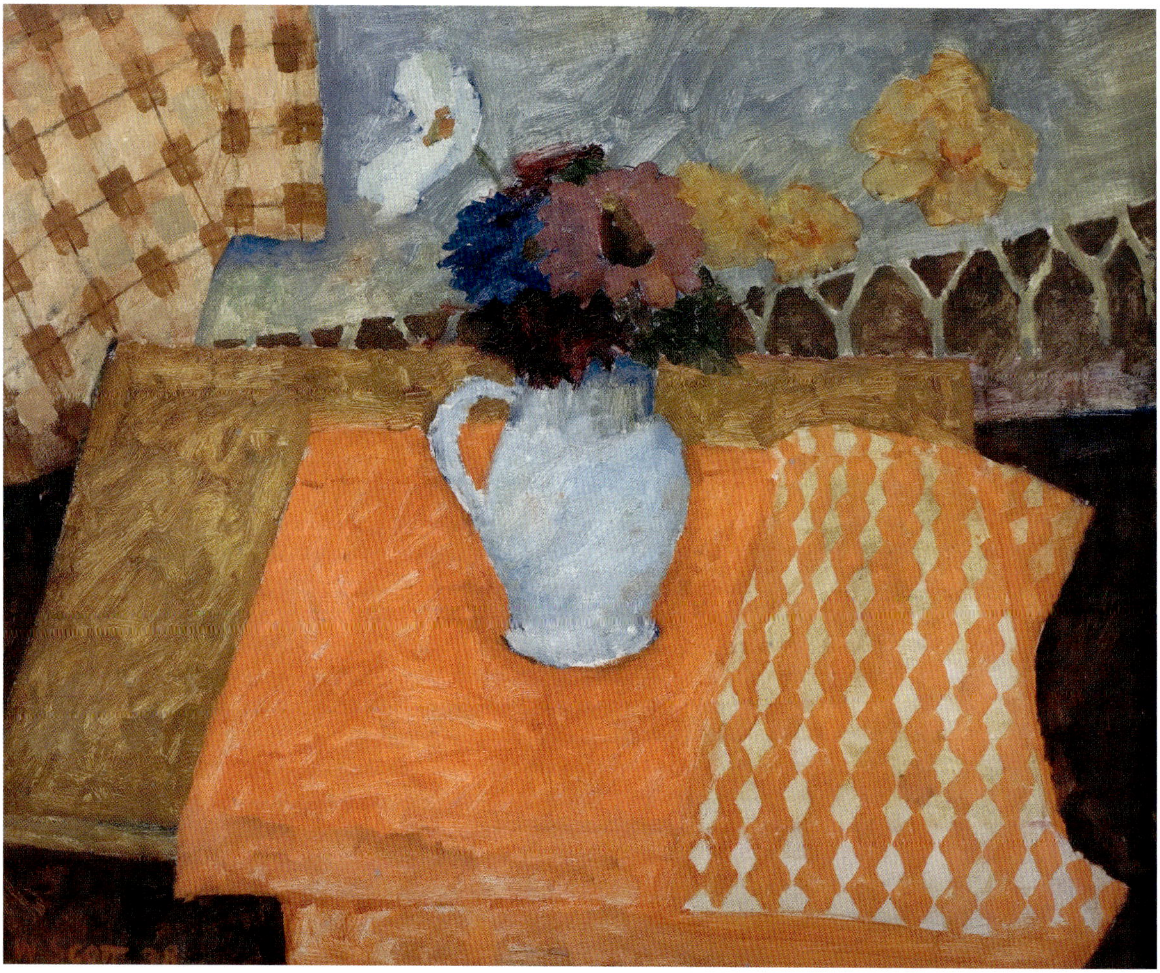

8

Flowers with Red Drapery

1938

Oil on canvas

51 x 61

Private collection

for Corot, Cézanne, Pierre Bonnard and George Stubbs. He would have come across the first three artists in reproductions as he rifled through the books on modern French art in Kathleen Bridle's flat in Enniskillen. By now, however, he had seen those French painters at first hand. Several trips to Paris, including a week's honeymoon there in 1937, had opened up an astonishing visual richness. The shock of seeing Cézanne's characteristic blue at first hand is clearly visible in *Girl and Blue Table*, not least in the stripes of her dress, which are painted in ridges of blue pigment squeezed straight out of the tube (the subject owes something to Cézanne's series of card players). And even though Bonnard's great late still lifes lay in the future, Scott had seen enough of the artist's recent work for it to inspire the colour dissonances of *Flowers with Red Drapery*. But what of the odd man out, George Stubbs? The sparsely populated green landscape with simple buildings, the only sign of human habitation, in *Breton Landscape* is very much in the spirit of a composition by Stubbs, who, as Scott was later to say, was the one English painter who came nearest to his own work. In their various ways, all four of these paintings show the concern that was to remain at the centre of his work: how to develop a modern pictorial language that would allow him to follow his natural instinct for tonal painting. Early on he recognised the artists who would prove to be the best guides. As he said, an artist's first loves in painting are the ones that matter most, and the ones that stay with him for life.

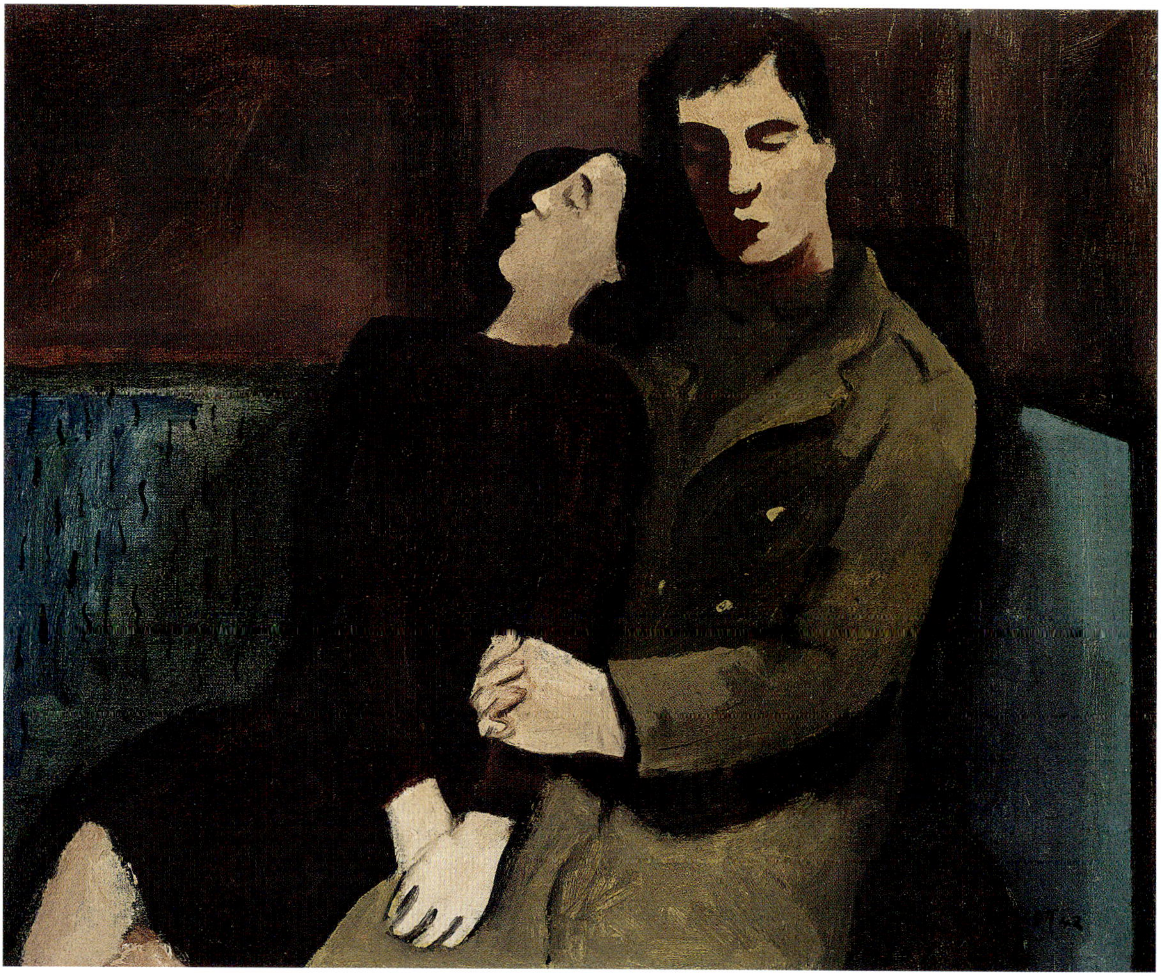

9

Soldier and Girl Sleeping

1942

Oil on canvas

41 x 50.9

Imperial War

Museum, London

2 'MY GUITAR'

ON THEIR RETURN from France in the late summer of 1939, the Scotts stayed in Dublin. William tried to find a teaching job there, but was repeatedly turned down because he could not speak the Irish language. So in March 1940, the couple left Ireland and moved back to London. The following year, with help from Mary's family, they completed their purchase of a cottage and farm in Somerset. Elm Tree Farm, in Hallatrow, was originally a traditional one-room-deep Somerset 'long house' with a stone slab floor in the entrance hallway. The end room of the building had been a stable with an apple store or hayloft above. Somerset, Scott was to say later, was one of the few parts of England where he felt at home. He had a profound antipathy to English gentility, which he associated with what he called 'flimsy black-and-white houses, snug cottages with roses round the door'. He chose to live in a part of the country that was, as he put it, 'less cleaned-up' than the Home Counties. Growing up in the austere surroundings of Greenock and Enniskillen had informed not only his painting, but his whole way of being.

Hallatrow was not far from Bath, where the local art school was run by a remarkable man, Clifford Ellis, by then a well-known graphic designer and soon to be a leading pioneer of postwar art education. Scott sought out Ellis, who immediately recognised his gifts as a painter and gave him a part-time teaching post. He arrived at an exceptional moment. Also teaching at the Bath School of Art one morning a week and free of charge was the elderly painter Walter Richard Sickert (one of those luminaries who had lent their name to Scott's painting school in Pont-Aven). He was living just outside Bath and eager to offer his services because, as he allegedly pointed out to Ellis, he was 'the only artist left in the world to have been acquainted with Degas, Manet, Monet and Whistler'. Sickert died in January 1942 at the age of eighty-one. Three months later, a particularly severe air raid over Bath during one weekend forced the school to abandon its premises. Sickert's widow, Thérèse Lessore, allowed Ellis's staff and students to move into the Sickerts' home at nearby Bathampton while they looked for new premises in Bath.

By the summer of 1942, however, Scott was faced with the prospect of being called up for active duty. He volunteered for the navy but was refused on physical grounds (he was five feet four inches in height and slightly built). Instead he enlisted in the army, where he served in the Royal Army Ordnance Corps. At first he had hopes of being appointed an official war artist, but these came to nothing. Ellis was on friendly terms with Kenneth Clark, the director of the National Gallery and an influential voice on the War Artists' Advisory Committee (Clark accepted Ellis's invitation to officially open the new premises of the Bath School of Art when it moved to Sydney Place, Bath, in November 1942). It was surely Ellis who asked Clark to intervene with the army on Scott's behalf. Moreover, Scott had recently been given his first London solo exhibition. This took place in September 1942 at the Leger Galleries in Old Bond Street and had attracted the attention of the painter John Piper, and the critic Clive Bell. With such a prestigious show under his belt, he had every reason to expect that he would be given the six months' leave to paint he had requested, or that some form of posting as a war artist would come his way. Clark, who said that he knew Scott's work and liked it, agreed to refer a letter to the War Office, but there the matter rested. The truth was that Scott's painting did not fit the conventions of official war art. How far it fell short is best summed up by a reviewer of *Soldiers' Verse*, an anthology of war poems illustrated by Scott (and published in 1945): 'The collection covers all aspects of the soldier's life, the flashing spear and tattered banners as well as bloodstains. The lithographs of William Scott, on the other hand, mostly convey only the bleak agony of war.'[9] As Clark and others on the War Artists' Advisory Committee knew better than most, at a time of national crisis spirits needed to be roused by a flash of steel rather than dampened by despondency.

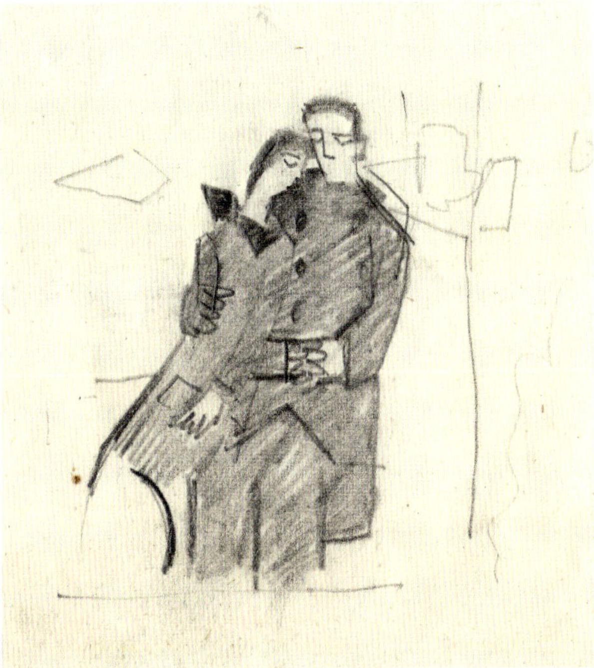

10
Study for **Soldier and Girl Sleeping**
1942
Pencil on paper
20 x 32
Private collection

In *Soldier and Girl Sleeping* (fig.9), which Clark must have seen at the Leger Galleries, Scott focuses on the exhaustion and weariness experienced by soldiers and civilians alike. The image of the soldier and his girlfriend asleep, drained by fatigue, could be seen as damagingly passive. In 1942, the committee was looking for art that expressed a nation's heroism in the face of a grave national threat: weariness smacked of defeatism.

On the false assumption that artists made good cartographers, a number of painters and graphic designers were posted to the map-making section of the Royal Engineers stationed at Wynnstay Hall, Ruabon, in north Wales. Scott arrived there in the spring of 1944. Conditions were primitive, not least because the owner of the house, Sir Watkin Williams-Wynn, refused to have water pipes laid to the camp, so the soldiers had to be taken in lorries to the mine at Tonypandy to wash in the miners' showers. But there were compensations. The commanding officer at Ruabon was sympathetic to the artists in his charge (who made pretty hopeless soldiers, as one of them, the painter Carel Weight, freely admitted). Those who asked permission were allowed time off to do their own work, and a sketching club was formed. Scott made the most of this relaxed regime by painting enough watercolours to earn him a second solo exhibition at the Leger Galleries in February 1945.

The war ended in August 1945 with the surrender of Japan, but Scott, like many others in the armed services, had to wait until January 1946 for demobilisation. His time at Ruabon had been productive, allowing him not only to store up a body of works on paper that he would exhibit later, but also to take advantage of the map-making facilities to learn the rudiments of printing. Nonetheless, the war left a terrible void. It was, said one art critic, 'a strange, unhappy moment' especially for those artists in Britain who before the war had looked to France for cultural impetus. Scott, having lived in Brittany for two years, felt the isolation from France particularly keenly. Picking up the pieces proved difficult.

Once the war was over, however, he disowned the series of watercolours he had shown at the Leger Galleries in 1945, regarding it as being too bound up with English romantic landscape painters, such as Piper, Michael Ayrton and Graham Sutherland. His reaction was almost certainly brought about by the shock of seeing what had been going on in France during the past five or six years. In December 1945 a major exhibition of Picasso and Matisse organised by L'Association Française d'Action Artistique and the British Council opened at the Victoria and Albert Museum in London. It included twenty-four wartime Picassos and earlier paintings by Matisse, mixed with the latter's interiors with figures painted during the war. Even though Scott was still in the army, a group visit to the exhibition was arranged by the Army Education Corps, one of a number of cultural expeditions intended to prepare soldiers for civilian life. In April of the following year, the Tate Gallery, now partially reopened after the wartime closure, held an exhibition of Georges Braque and Georges Rouault, an exhibition that affected Scott as profoundly as the Matisse and Picasso show. Seeing Picasso and Braque in particular, both masters of the still life, seems to have shaken Scott out of his temporary inertia. The impact made by these two artists is clearly visible in *Mackerel with Plate and Paper* 1946 (fig.11) in which the shapes made the layers of paper combined with a round white plate put formal considerations before the subject. The fish are wrapped in greaseproof paper, the sharp lines of which contrast with the irregular outline of the white cloth beneath. The fish and the cloth are separated by the oval of the plate that rests on top of a frying pan. The shapes are so cleanly defined they might have been cut out of paper. The carefully modulated play with shape is subtly continued in the sleek curves of the two mackerel, which rhyme with the two curved sides of the half-hidden plate. Building up a still life in a series of flat layers is a

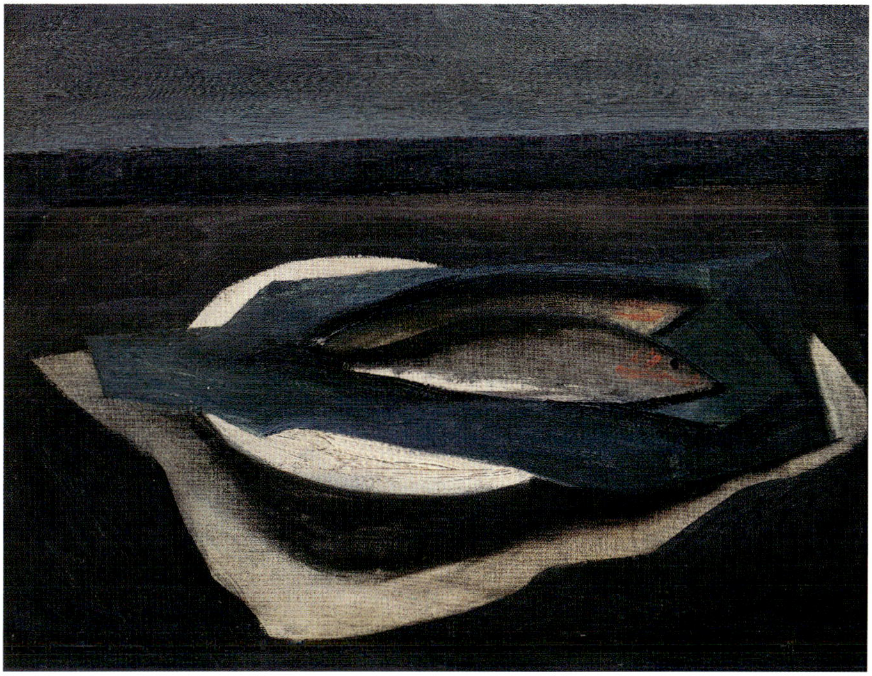

11
Mackerel with Plate and Paper
1946
Oil on canvas
40.8 x 50.8
Private collection

method of working that owes much to Braque, while the blacks, dark blues and whites echo the sombre light of a wartime still life by Picasso.

Half-hidden under the china plate in *Mackerel with Plate and Paper* is the frying pan, the object that, as Scott announced, would be for him what the guitar was to Picasso and Braque. Being essentially a straight line ending in a generously rounded form, the frying pan is, in purely formal terms, a close equivalent to the guitar. Indeed, when hung upright on a wall (as it appears in Scott's later work), the frying pan can be seen to mimic the role of the cubist guitar. In 1952, writing to an unidentified friend known only as 'George' (possibly a fellow student from art school), Scott explained the genesis of his frying pan pictures: 'About four years [sic] ago I painted a picture of a frying pan and a white napkin. I had been interested in the works of Braque for a long time but I felt that it was dishonest to merely take as some people have done the guitar, the carafe and the French loaf. I felt that in painting my own familiar objects I might imbue them with a conviction characteristic of both myself and my race, if the guitar was to Braque his Madonna the frying pan would be my guitar. Black was a colour I was fond of and I possessed at that moment a very black pan. I painted my first picture of a frying pan and napkin (fig.12), it was entirely a work of visual observation. I became entranced with the shape it made on a white cloth.'[10] The emphasis Scott lays on the importance of being faithful not only to himself but to his 'race' might strike some as curious, but his words were carefully chosen. By 'race' he was identifying with the people of Scotland and Northern Ireland with whom he had been raised (a London friend who knew him well once remarked that Scott, a sociable man, never felt entirely comfortable in a room full of people unless he came across a fellow Celt).[11] The frying pan was the object he associated with growing up in Enniskillen, where fish was the staple food and a large pan blackened with use was the most commonly seen piece of kitchen equipment. However, his assertion that *The Frying Pan* was 'entirely a work of visual observation' is less credible. The white cloth is folded as crisply as a piece of linen in a still life by Zurbarán, and so arranged that a small triangle of white appears from under the large cloth, each corner of which forms a triangle of a different size. The folds are as carefully manipulated as a piece of origami. The relationship of the three objects is also carefully considered. They are not so much distinct elements of a still life, as might be found in an old master painting, but objects that relate to each other in a curiously human way. As Scott said some years later, 'I wanted to animate a still life in the sense that one could animate a figure'[12] (a remark that reflects his experience of Picasso's still lifes with their powerful human overtones). The relationship of the large black frying pan with the delicate ceramic bowl suggests a male and female couple (united by their two shadows, which merge together in one dark pool), while the prongs of the toasting fork introduce a note of spikiness, echoing the crispness of the folded linen.

There were other reasons for choosing the most ordinary objects, even though these were, as Scott liked to stress, completely without interest. 'That's why I paint them', he once declared, 'They convey nothing. There is no meaning to them at all but they are a means to making a picture ... They are abstract, these paintings, as a still life by Chardin is abstract.'[13] The way he uses objects both as pure form and as metaphors for emotions such as tenderness, closeness, and sexual desire, has no parallel in British art of the period. As he explained in 1959, 'I'm surrounded by the objects I paint. I don't actually lay them out on a table and paint from them anymore. They are in my studio as presences, watching me at work, as if they were a number of little sculptures' (an attitude to the inanimate object that is reminiscent of the 'magical' quality that Picasso, for instance, invested in the African masks and fetishes he collected and kept in his studio).

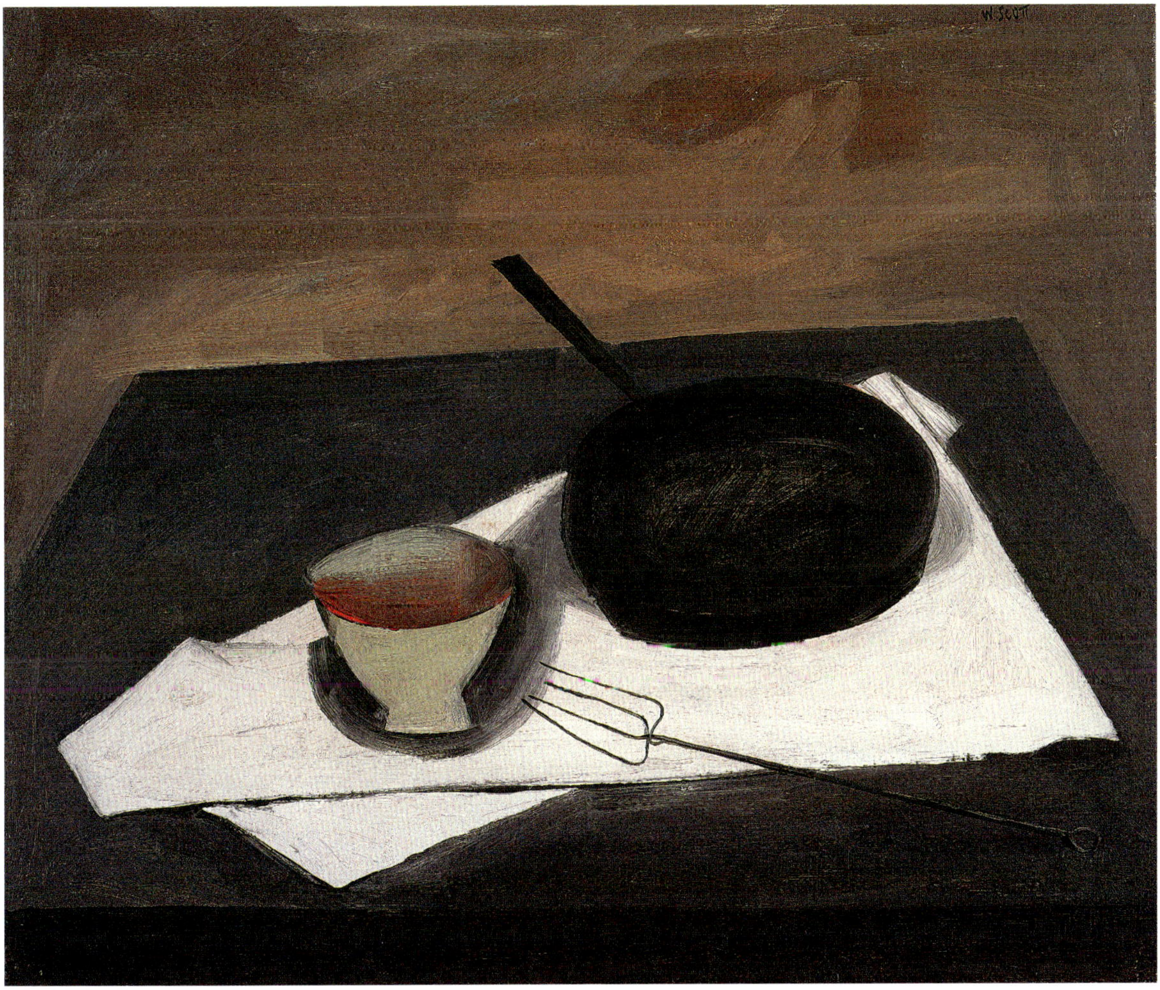

12
The Frying Pan
1946
Oil on canvas
54.5 x 65.1
Arts Council Collection,
Southbank Centre, London

Even though a few outstanding British painters, such as Ben Nicholson and Christopher Wood, played their part in Scott's early formation, his instinct was to look to France rather than to England. Even as he was painting radical still lifes such as *Mackerel with Plate and Paper* and *The Frying Pan*, he was again turning to one of his favourite painters. *Girl in a Striped Skirt* (fig.13) is virtually copied from a painting by Corot,[14] a reproduction of which he had cut out of a book and kept. Scott's remark that his own paintings were abstract 'as a still life by Chardin is abstract' is relevant even in this traditional figurative painting, in which he brings the figure right to the foreground, flattening the planes and obliterating detail. The same respect for tradition is seen in *Hare and Candle* (fig.14), a still life in which the dead hare and the extinguished candle refer explicitly to the subject

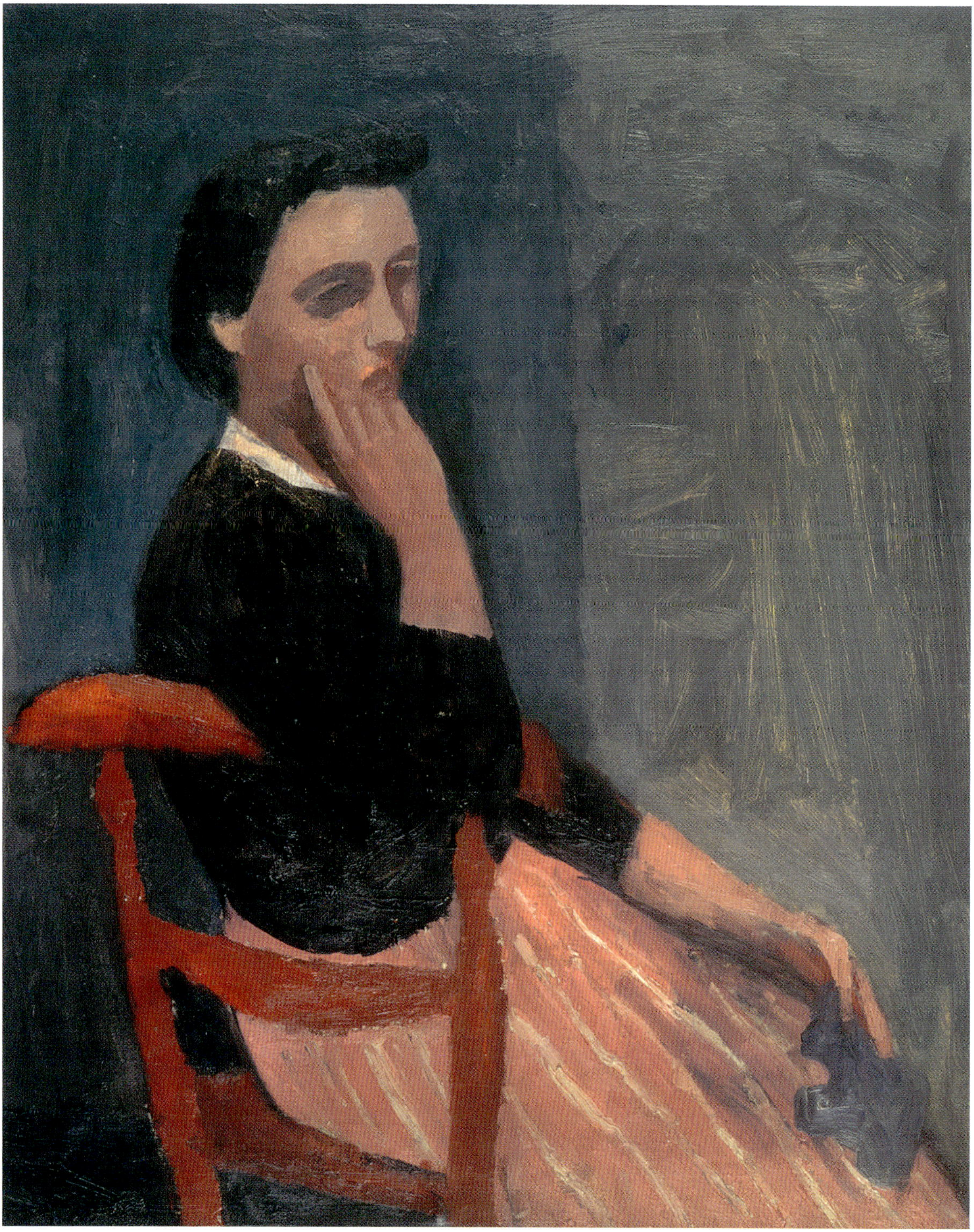

matter of Dutch and Flemish old masters. No painting better illustrates the intention Scott later stated in the catalogue of his retrospective exhibition at the Tate Gallery in 1972: 'I wanted to look at Cézanne not through cubist eyes but rather through the eyes of Chardin.' The way the table tilts up and towards the viewer is a device he borrowed from Cézanne, while the prominence given to the stiffened body of the hare recalls the prominence Chardin gave to the dead fish in his celebrated painting *The Skate*, a work that Scott knew well from his visits to the Louvre.

No more than a year separates *Hare and Candle* from *Table Still Life* 1951 (fig.15), but in that short time a new level of confidence emerged. In 1951, in preparation for the Festival of Britain, a postwar celebration of British design, a number of artists, including Scott, were invited to participate in *Sixty Paintings for '51*, a touring exhibition organised by the Arts Council of Great Britain with the aim of encouraging corporate patronage of the visual arts. The exhibition had a practical purpose: to discover a new type of art for public spaces – works to hang 'in a new church, a modern liner, the offices of the National Coal Board, the hotel lounges of British Railways, the waiting rooms of airports, the foyers of cinemas'.[15] The ambition behind the scheme was reflected in the size of the paintings demanded of the artists. For Scott, the commission gave him the opportunity to sum up, as it were, the series of frying pan pictures he had begun in 1946, but on a new scale. That painting, *Still Life* 1951, did not come easily, largely because the change of scale demanded more than just making the composition bigger: as Scott put it, 'I had to create something that was myself on a larger scale.' But out of it came a second, even larger work, *Table Still Life*, in which the artist achieved his aim of realising more fully the abstract relationship of form and space. As he told his (unidentified) friend George in the letter cited above, he had always considered himself a figure painter, a surprising remark coming from an artist who is best known for reinventing the still life, but it is clear from his own description of the Festival of Britain picture, where he likens the handle of the frying pan to an arm stretching across the picture, that he wanted a still life to have the human properties of a figure painting. The handle had another function – to help flatten the picture plane. And flatness was all-important. 'All kinds of pictures that I like in the world seem to be flat', he said. 'Apart from all primitive art I like the first beginnings of European art. I like the Byzantines, I like the early Italians and then there are great gaps in my liking of painting until we come to

13
Girl in a Striped Skirt
1946
Oil on canvas
61 x 48.2
Private collection

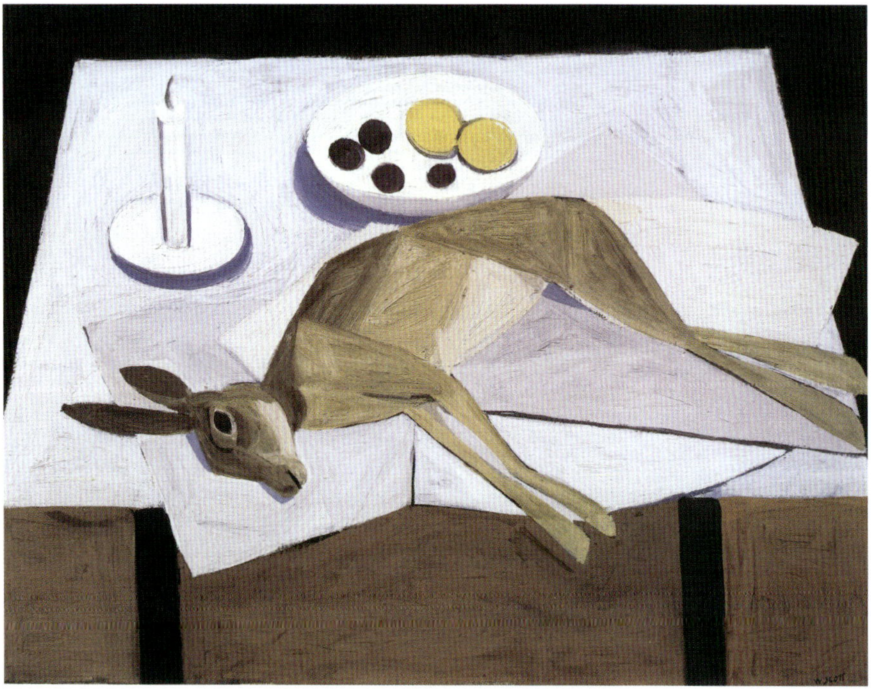

14
Hare and Candle
1949 or 1950
Oil on canvas
66.4 x 81.4
Private collection

Cézanne.'[16] On one level, the tabletop, now tilted vertically and supported by five 'legs' (the extra one is deliberately misplaced), has the look of a highly schematic rendering of a body, with arms extending either side, and a tall thin coffee pot representing the head placed top centre (it does not take too much imagination to see this image as a distant echo of one of the Byzantine Crucifixions he admired). The construction of *Table Still Life* is thoroughly assured, partly because the play on the double image is conducted with great concision as well as subtlety (the body and the still life can be read simultaneously), and partly because the table is as solid as a piece of sculpture, the arms and legs acting like a metal armature, with the white slab of the table itself laid on like a piece of plaster (the white paint has the look of roughly handled plaster). (It may be relevant that just at the time Scott was painting both the Festival *Still Life* and *Table Still Life*, he was introduced to the sculptor F.E. McWilliam, who was then working on large sculptures for the Festival of Britain celebrations: the two artists, both from Northern Ireland, became lifelong friends.)

Although Scott had little time for surrealism (a movement that had played a significant part in British art of the 1930s), it is hard not to see his taste for the ambiguous image as being related to the kind of play on the Freudian thinking

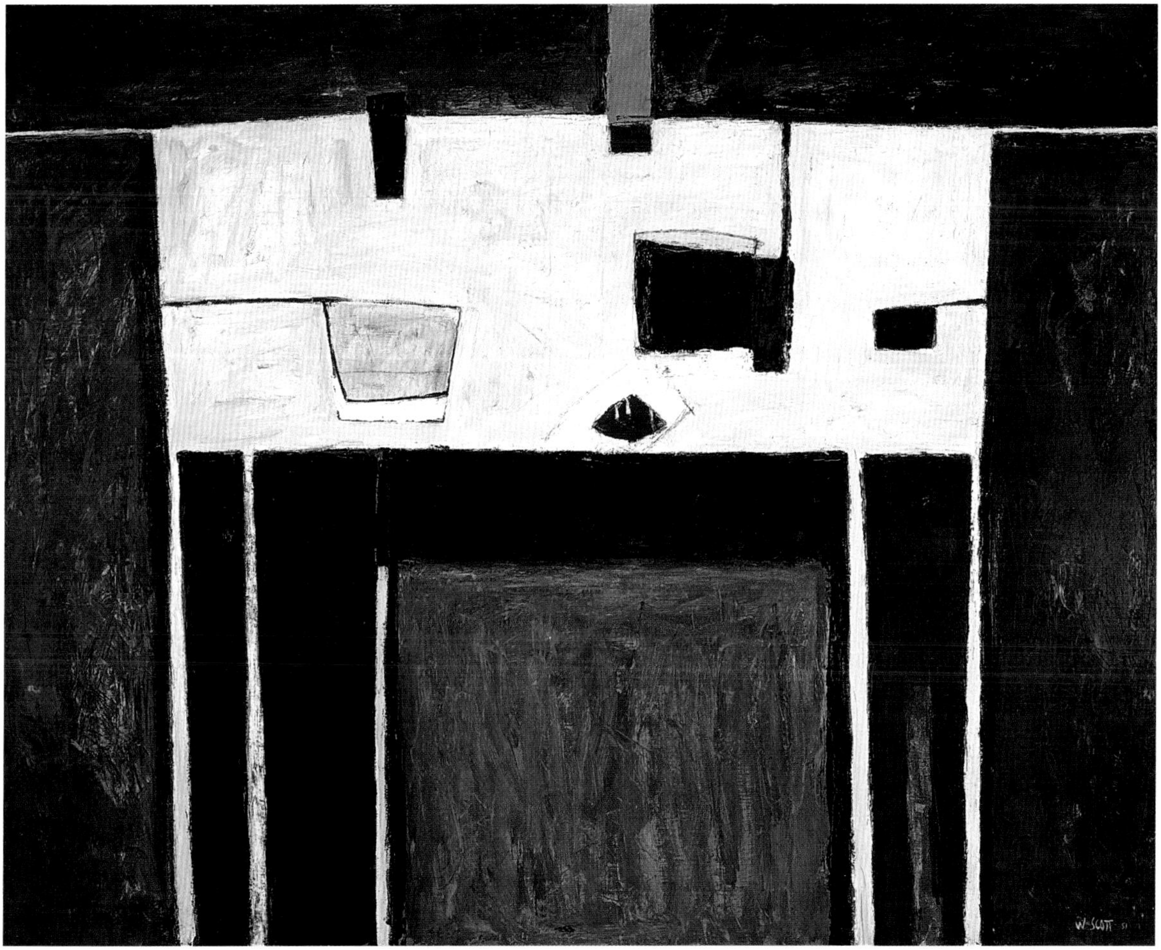

15
Table Still Life
1951
Oil on canvas
143.3 x 183.8
British Council Collection

that had influenced so many creative minds of the period. *The Harbour* 1952 (fig.16), for instance, is a master class in ambiguity. The painter Patrick Heron (a close friend of Scott's) was responding to the picture's ambivalent nature when he admitted to being 'alarmed by the animal vigour of the image', a reference to the powerful thrust of the strong black line of the harbour jetty. The title dictates the way one sees the painting at first, but if one stays a while in front of the image, the small black square tucked into the left-hand corner soon converts the white space into a body and the curving jetty into an arm: suddenly the image is no longer a landscape but a reclining figure. Push the interpretation one step further and the painting can be seen as a perfect double image in which the male (represented by the penetrating line of the jetty) and the female are seen both separately and together. As Heron pointed out, 'the thick, knifed, white pigment everywhere has, in conjunction with the black,

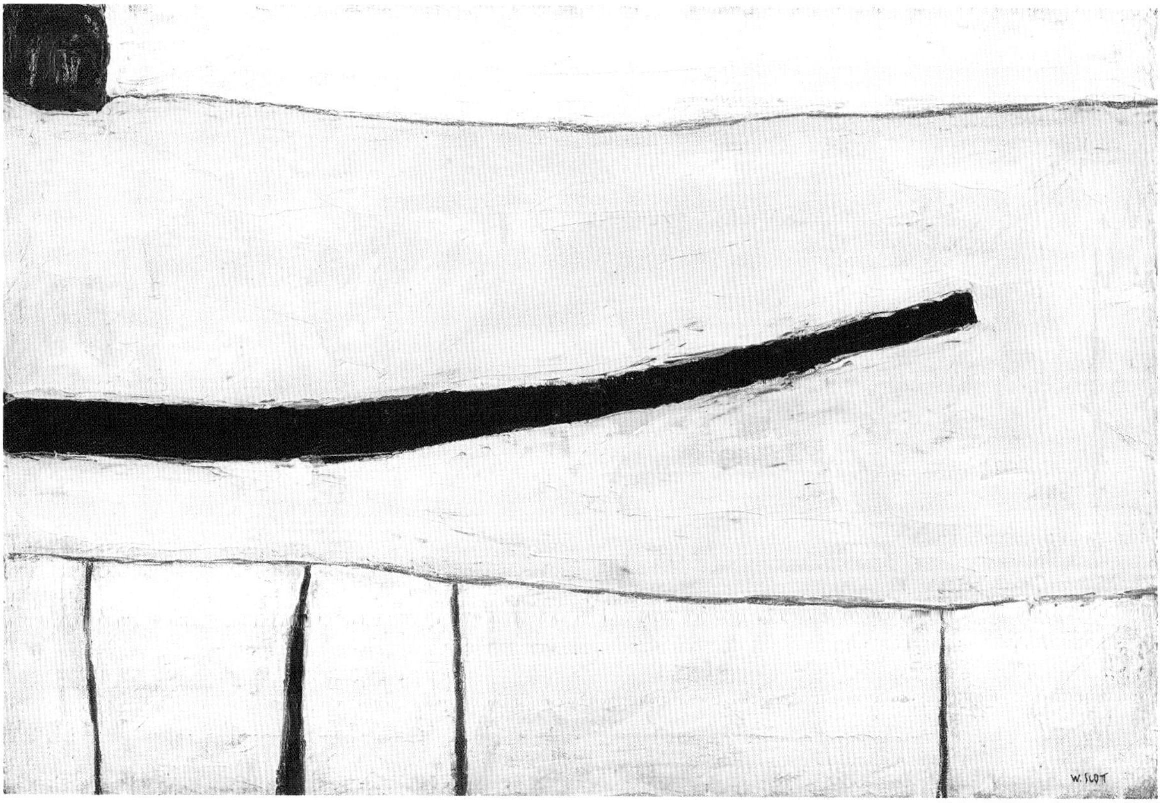

16
The Harbour
1952
Oil on canvas
61.3 x 91.7
Tate

a positive voluptuousness'. The painting looks austere, but when seen close up, the layering of pure whites and dirty whites reveals that sensuousness of touch.

There were other ambiguities to help Scott steer his subject away from the literal: for instance, a flat white surface placed at the centre of the canvas can be read as a tabletop, a flattened torso or an expanse of water. Look at *The Harbour* and then look again at *Table Still Life*, where the objects anchored to the edges of the table cease to be pots and pans and become boats moored in a harbour. Using an almost monochrome palette for the works of the early 1950s helped Scott, so he said, to find solutions to structural problems and released him, so he claimed, 'of responsibilities and struggles with colour'. 'I limited my colour to the use almost entirely of blacks and greys and the search for greater space. I no longer wanted my pictures to be a collection of objects related spatially but to be an object with a presence in its own right.' Whereas a still life such as *Mackerel with Plate and Paper* was painted from life, *Table Still Life*, less closely tied to the motif, is composed of images stored in the imagination. As Scott now recognised, subjects such as the figure, still life or landscape could happily merge with one another until they became almost indivisible.

Even though the argument of figurative art versus abstraction may appear rather irrelevant to an audience today, it was real enough to British artists of the early 1950s, particularly to artists of Scott's generation who had emerged from the Second World War feeling out of touch and with only a hazy sense of direction. By 1952 the question had become a pressing one. One of the most significant events that year was the series of three exhibitions of abstract art organised by the painter Adrian Heath in his studio at 22 Fitzroy Street, the first of which took place in March. This followed an exhibition of paintings by the French painter Nicolas de Staël that had opened at the Matthiesen Gallery in New Bond Street a few weeks earlier. Scott, who visited the de Staël exhibition with Heron, encountered a style of painting he could immediately relate to: forceful, gritty and unrefined. The surfaces of de Staël's paintings, which look as though they have been constructed out of slabs of masonry, appealed to Scott's taste for the rough-hewn. It was this encounter with de Staël's painting that prompted an outpouring of abstract gouaches realised that summer (figs.17–18).[17] Gouache, a more spontaneous medium than oils, was also a way for Scott to feel his way back into colour. One of the lessons he learned from de Staël was to think of paint as plaster, roughly layering it on and scraping it into shape as though using a trowel rather than a brush (his experience of working in plaster as a sculpture student is never wholly absent in his more heavily worked paintings). However, the artists who had shown at the first two weekend exhibitions in Heath's studio, the London-based 'Constructionists' such as Anthony Hill, Kenneth and Mary Martin, Robert Adams and Victor Pasmore, were uncompromising when it came to banishing the marks of the 'handmade'. This changed when Heath organised the third and last exhibition of abstract art and invited three other painters to participate: Scott, Terry Frost (who had been in a prisoner of war camp with Heath) and Roger Hilton, a choice of artists that offered a broader and more painterly idea of abstraction. By taking part in this exhibition, which was the most representative of the three as it included works in various media, Scott was recognised as a painter in the vanguard of abstraction.

Essential to Scott's work of the 1950s was his position as senior painting master at the renamed Bath Academy of Art, a post he took up in the autumn of 1946, thanks again to Clifford Ellis. Like so many artists of his generation, he was unable to survive on what little money he made from

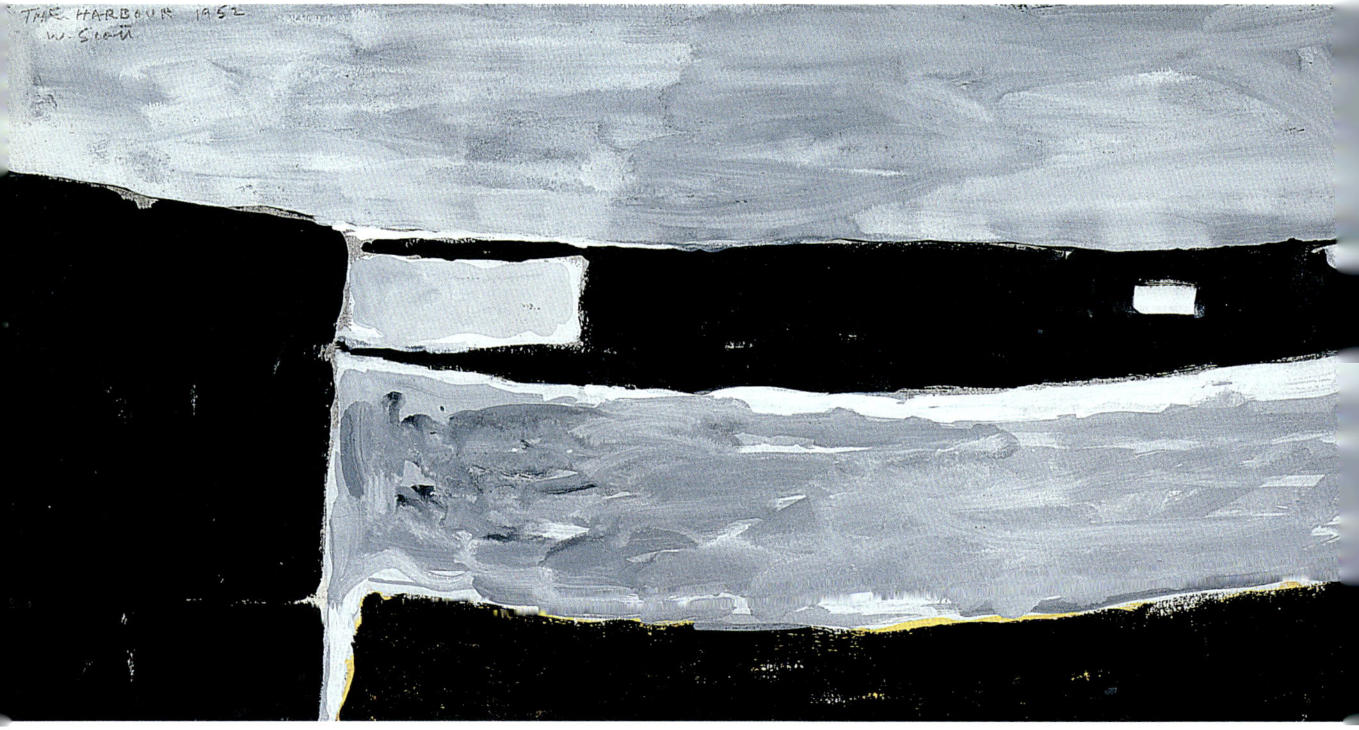

17
The Harbour
1952
Gouache on paper
20.3 x 38.5
Private collection

selling his work; he needed regular employment, and continued to depend on teaching until he was in his late forties. While many artists might find teaching a drudgery, Scott seems to have thrived on it. Ellis, who aimed to provide his students with a liberal education, saw to it that the teaching was conducted within the framework of 'an environment which is itself an expression of a civilized way of living'. That environment was created by moving the school from Bath to Corsham Court in Wiltshire, the ancestral home of Lord Methuen (and the reason the school is always referred to as Corsham). The circumstances were ideal, particularly for students growing up in the austerity of postwar Britain. The handsome surroundings of the Court and its extensive grounds were the backdrop to the painting and sculpture studios and workshops housed in the stables, barns and outhouses. Scott was able to do a lot of his own work at Corsham (where he had his own studio, jealously guarded, so it is said), but that was all part of the ethos of the school. Ellis was adamant that his students should work alongside professional artists. He encouraged a close relationship between the staff and students chiefly because he wanted the students to experience the dedication of the seriously committed artist. Not only that, but the artists worked in a variety of disciplines, so that painters like Scott and

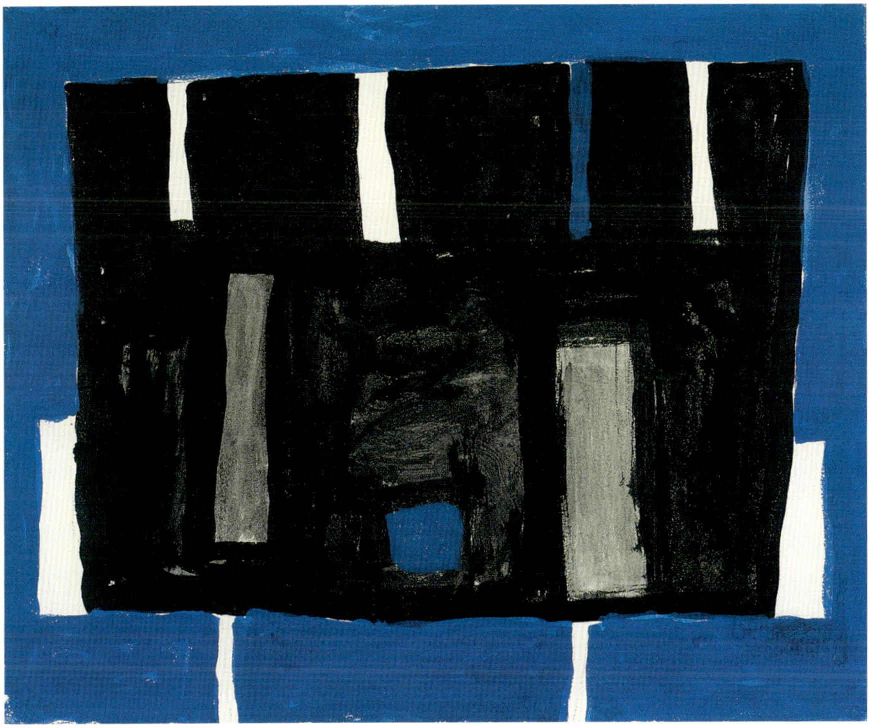

18
Untitled
1952
Gouache on paper
38 x 47.5
Richard Green Fine
Paintings, London

Peter Lanyon, for example, would take the opportunity to work with the potter James Tower or the sculptor Bernard Meadows.

It is not always the most powerful or successful artist who exerts the strongest influence. The roll-call of artists working at Corsham, names such as Lanyon, Kenneth Armitage, Terry Frost and Lynn Chadwick, conjures up a select group of the exceptionally talented, but it has to be remembered that in the early 1950s these were artists relatively cut off from art outside their own country. It is true that modern masters such as Picasso, Matisse, Braque and Klee could be seen in London dealers' galleries, as well as in important official exhibitions, but new work from France and elsewhere was thin on the ground (hence Scott's excitement at seeing de Staël's paintings at the Matthiesen Gallery). Nor is all new art discovered at first hand. So it was that both staff and students at Corsham learned about the art of Jean Dubuffet and *art brut* through the example of a young French student who arrived at Corsham some time in 1951. Marie-Christine Treinen was the daughter of a wealthy banker living on the outskirts of Paris, and it was probably through the friendship of Ellis's wife Rosemary (a distinguished designer and illustrator) with a French art teacher, Madame Vigé Langevin, that led the young Paris student to accept a place at Corsham. From the moment she arrived, Treinen was brimming over with confidence. Whatever she did – painting, drawing, sculpture – she did on an impressively grand scale, so grand that she thought nothing of invading every available studio space. Her method of painting, for example, was to spread sheets of brown paper on the floor and paint enormous figures with sweeping strokes of the brush. To students working with A4 sketch pads and small canvases, the directness of her attack – on the figure in particular – was new, and unnerving. It was not only the students who found themselves 'rattled' (the word used by the painter Paul Feiler to describe the effect Treinen had on the staff and students alike).[18] Scott and Lanyon never disguised their admiration for her boldness and originality. Other members of staff to take her seriously were the sculptors Armitage and Chadwick. The few known works by Treinen (oils, lithographs and ceramics) do not really live up to her Corsham legend, but that is not the point. The timing of her arrival at the school, bringing with her some first-hand knowledge of the raw unpolished work of *art brut*, combined with her own uninhibited, almost primitive, approach to painting and her extrovert attitude guaranteed that she would leave her mark. Bernard Meadows, for instance, described her influence at Corsham as 'tremendous'. Those who were around at the time could see a strong link between the way she rejected modelling by flattening out the torso (like one of Dubuffet's steam-rollered nudes) and the way her teachers followed her lead: Scott in a series of nudes, and Armitage in his bronzes. No photograph of Treinen has been found, but her memory is fleetingly commemorated in a painting by Howard Hodgkin (a fellow student at Corsham): she is seen in top right in *Interior of a Museum* (Tate), her hair tied in a knot.[19]

The Frying Pan
1946 (detail of fig.12)

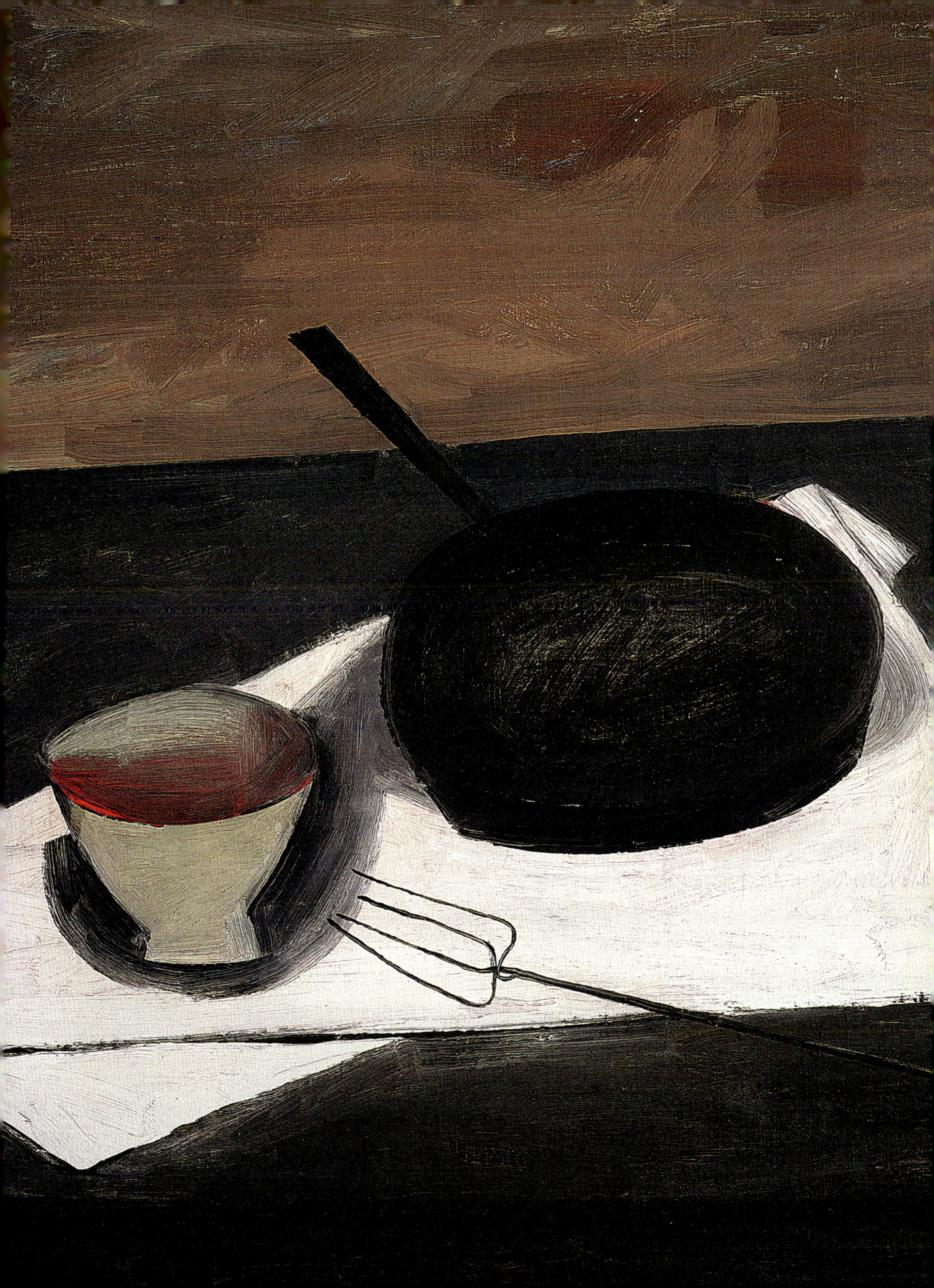

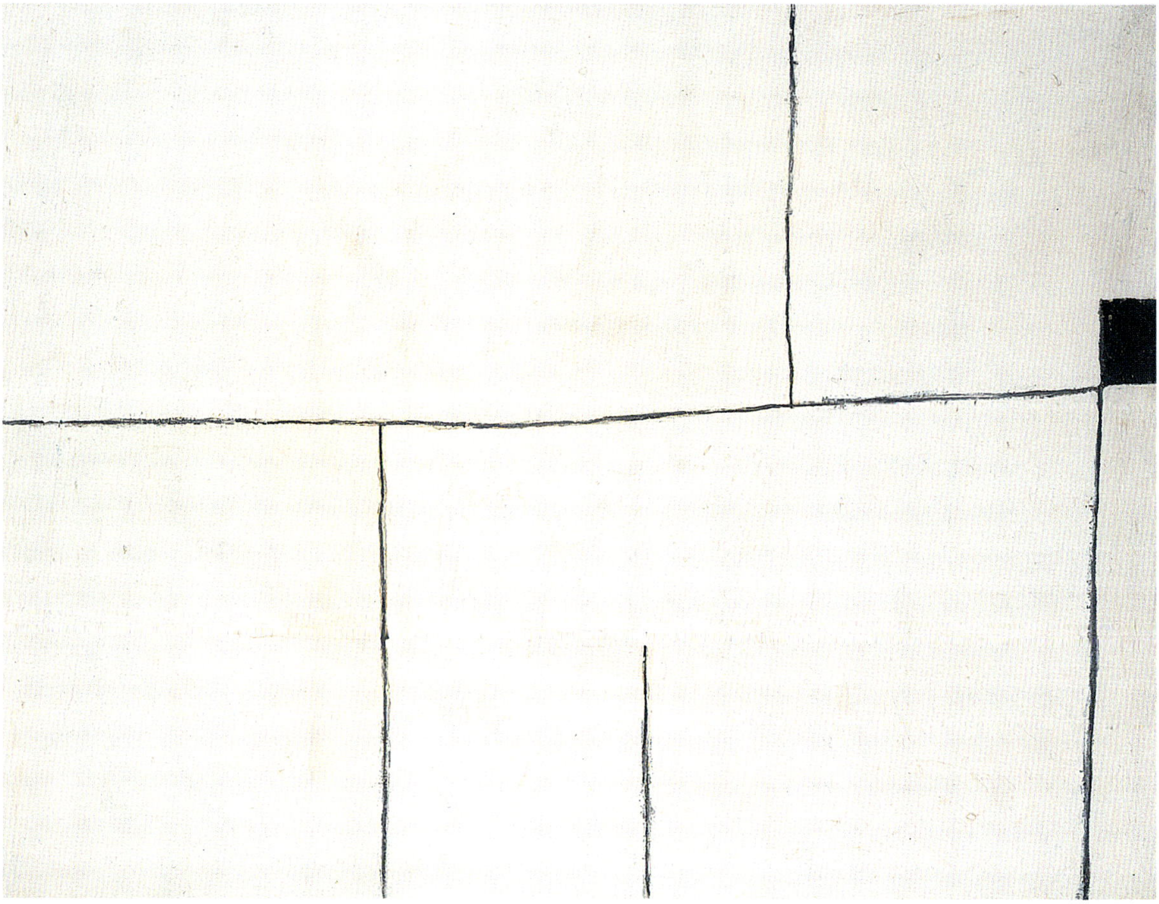

19

Figure into Landscape

1953

Oil on canvas

114.3 x 152.4

Private collection

3 A MOMENT OF TRANSITION

AT THE TIME of Scott's first solo exhibition at the Hanover Gallery in June 1953, his name would have been familiar to any regular visitor to the London art galleries. Patrick Heron described him as 'one of our small handful of really significant painters', a tribute to the recent series of abstracts such as *The Harbour* and *Figure into Landscape* (figs.16 and 19), which were recognised for the groundbreaking works they were. Teaching at Corsham gave Scott the companionship of like-minded artists, but in London he belonged to what he described as 'a very small band of British abstract artists much ridiculed by our critics and given few opportunities for showing our work'. His words were carefully chosen. A band is not the same as a group, and while he and painters such as Victor Pasmore and Adrian Heath shared an interest in the work of Ben Nicholson, that was about all: they were drawn together more by a sense of common purpose in the face of what Scott described as a 'general hostility' to abstraction than by commonly held beliefs. *Orange, Black and White Composition* 1953 (fig.20), painted at the same time as Scott was concentrating on black-and-white abstractions, suggests that when thinking about colour in abstract terms he was conscious of Nicholson's work of the mid-1930s, the moment when the older artist was absorbing the work of Piet Mondrian. Although the shapes in *Orange, Black and White Composition* are roughly and unevenly painted, and straight lines studiously avoided, the way the black ground cuts into the main composition indicates

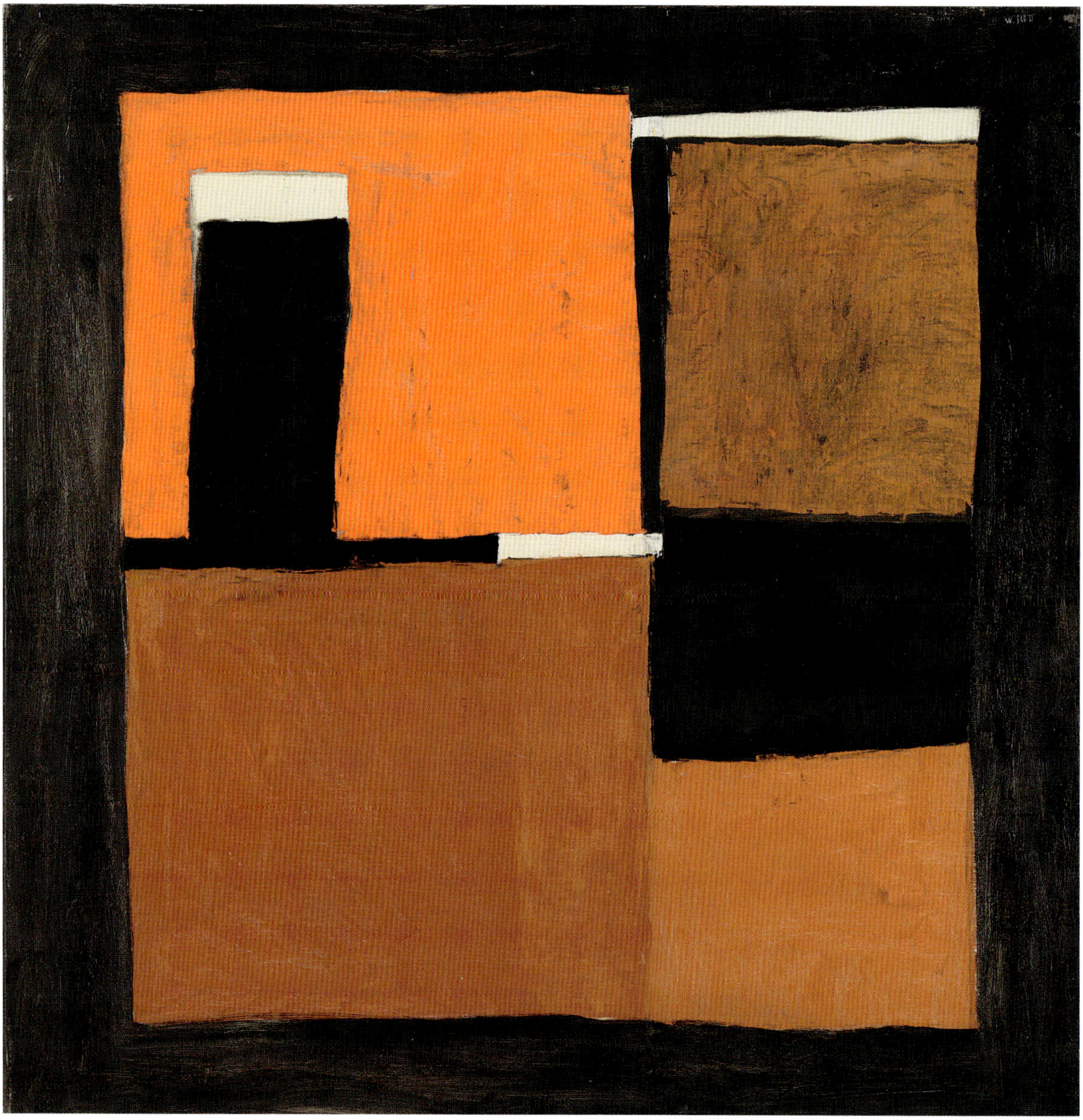

20

Orange, Black and White Composition
1953
Oil on canvas

121.9 x 121.9
Tate. Presented by the Trustees of the Chantrey Bequest 1966

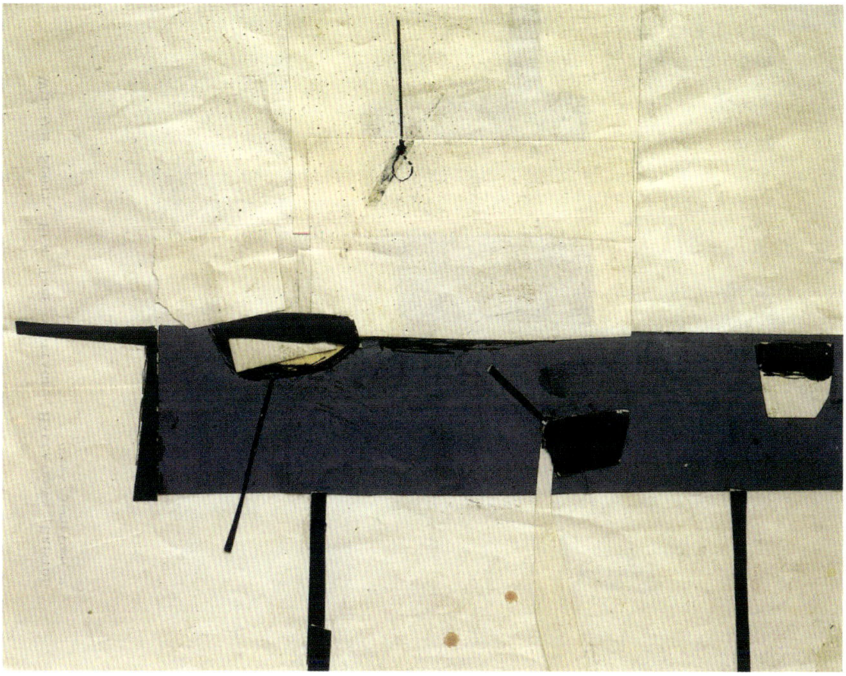

21
Untitled
c.1951
Pasted paper and pencil on paper
20.5 x 25.5
Private collection

the close attention Scott paid to Nicholson. And cutting may well have played a literal part in the making of *Orange, Black and White Composition.* Scott is known to have experimented with irregularly cut pieces of paper, trying them out on the canvas prior to picking up a brush. It was, so to speak, the equivalent of making a preparatory drawing (fig.21). As noted earlier, even in an early still life such as *Mackerel with Plate and Paper*, the sharply outlined forms look as though they had been fashioned with a pair of scissors.

A few months after his show opened at the Hanover Gallery, Scott left for Canada to spend several weeks as a guest lecturer at the Banff School of Fine Arts at the University of Alberta, Canada, an arrangement set up by the British Council. Scott was following in the footsteps of two English painters previously invited to teach at Banff, Edward Bawden and William Townsend, but, as he was to find out, Banff was not like Corsham. And Banff was to find out that Scott was not like Bawden or Townsend. In a letter to the British Council explaining why Scott would not be invited back for a second visit (as was the custom) the principal of Banff reflected that while the painter's predilection for modern art was 'quite right and proper', it gave the impression of a rigid frame of mind. In other words, modernism would be tolerated at Banff, but only if diluted with a large dose of traditional values.

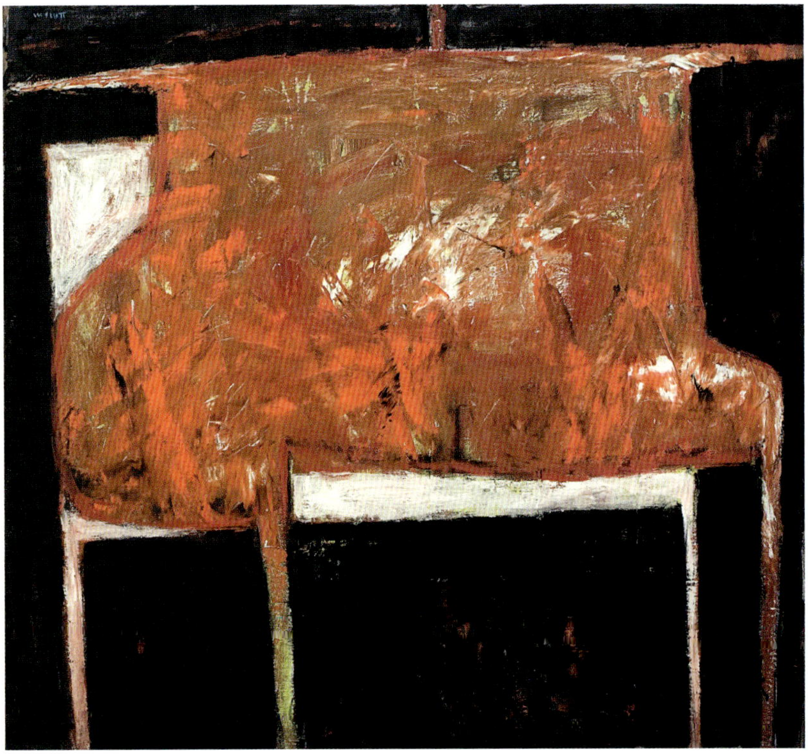

22
Figure: Red and Black
1954
Oil on canvas
89 x 99
Private collection

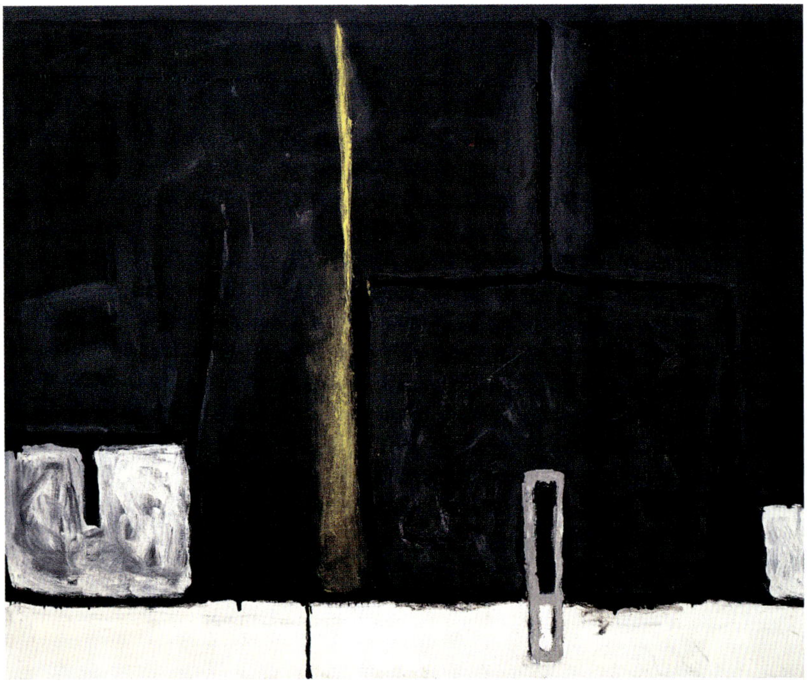

23
Composition III
1955
Oil on canvas
86.5 x 106
Private collection

The journey to Canada, however, was far from wasted. Before returning to England Scott travelled to New York, where Martha Jackson, an enterprising art dealer with a special interest in European artists, invited him to stay in her gallery at 22 East 66th Street. Jackson, who was to represent Scott in America from 1955 until her death in 1969, set about introducing him to the New York art world. Scott cannot have stayed much longer than four or five days, but within that brief time he met Mark Rothko, Franz Kline, Willem de Kooning and Jackson Pollock. He spent several days on Long Island, where Jackson had a house, and it was there that he probably met de Kooning, who had set up a temporary studio on the porch of a house owned by the art dealer Leo Castelli (several photographs taken there show Scott standing in front of an unfinished 'Woman' by de Kooning).[20] He also visited the painter Alfonso Ossorio, who had acquired Dubuffet's original collection of *art brut*. This first experience of the New York art world was, as he later said, 'a surprise and a shock'. The Americans had discovered what Scott later described as the 'right scale' for abstract painting. 'I was overwhelmed by its audacity and technical skill. Here I thought was a public art and an art that was right for America. My reaction to American painting was, I think, to make me realize that my origin was in Europe.'[21] When Scott returned from America he looked again at the abstract paintings he had recently shown at the Hanover Gallery and came to the conclusion that there was no reason for him to continue down that road. 'My experience in America gave me a determination to re-paint much that I had left unfinished in terms of the symbolic still life. With the example of Ben Nicholson, whom I much admired, there was no reason for me to be devoted solely to abstraction and I embarked on a process of re-discovery.'[22] Scott was only too aware of the English critics' hostility to abstraction, so he must have been pleased to learn from Jackson that he had at least one influential admirer in America: James Johnson Sweeney, director of the Solomon R. Guggenheim Museum, who had spoken highly of Scott's work, reportedly exclaiming, 'At last England has a painter!'[23] These were not empty words: in December Sweeney included Scott in his *Younger European Painters* show at the Guggenheim, the only British artist to be represented.

Once back in England, Scott set about rediscovering both the still life and the figure. *Figure: Red and Black* 1954 (fig.22) echoes the large tablet form of *Table Still Life*, but with none of its austerity. The experience of seeing one of de Kooning's 'Women' at close quarters may account for the brazen frontality of this nude, but her splayed form and meaty texture owes just as much to Dubuffet's paintings of women that Scott had seen at Ossorio's

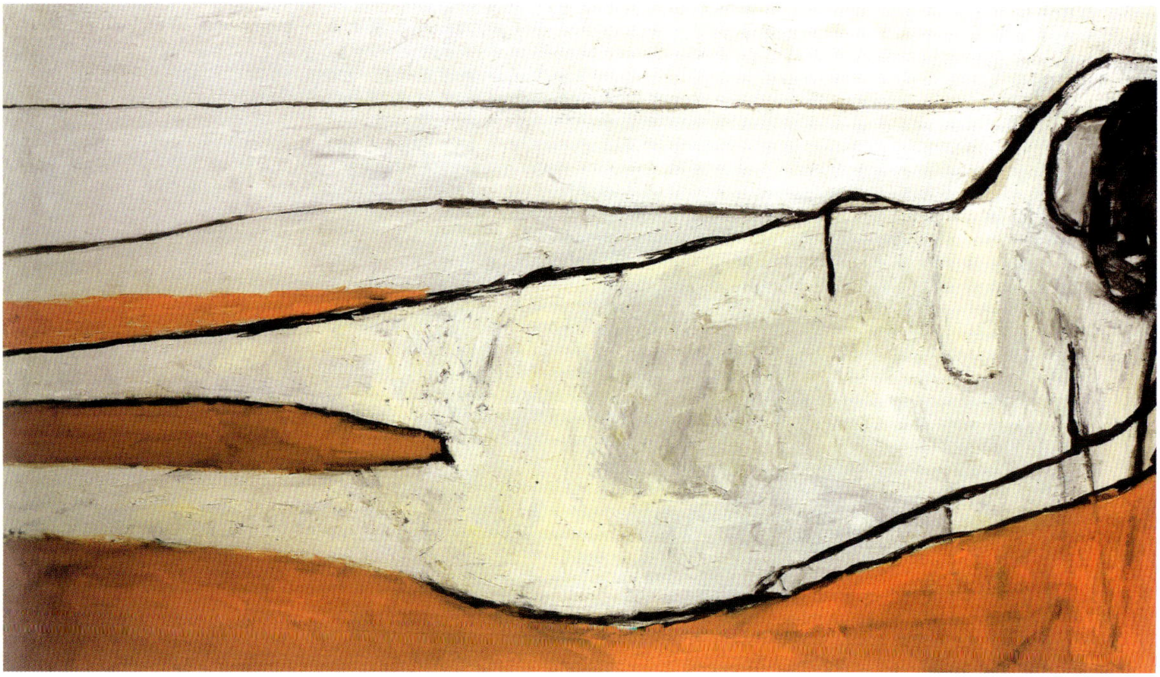

24
White Reclining Nude
1956
Oil on canvas
91.8 x 152.7
Hirshhorn Museum and Sculpture Garden, Smithsonian Institution, The Martha Jackson Memorial Collection: Gift of Mr and Mrs David K Anderson, 1980

house in East Hampton the same weekend (maybe even on the same day) he stood in de Kooning's makeshift studio in the Hamptons. The nude is all flesh (reproduction cannot do justice to the juicy reds and oranges of the woman's body), while her head and limbs are as sticklike as the legs of the chair. De Kooning and Dubuffet both offered superlative examples of how figure painting was far from dead (as the more purist defenders of abstraction liked to believe), but there was another artist whose work mattered as much to Scott, if not more. It can happen, and indeed often does, that an artist responds as enthusiastically to a fellow artist's temperament and personality as to the art. So it was with Scott and Rothko. Living on opposite sides of the Atlantic, they met rarely (and Scott was no letter writer), but the bond between the two was both affectionate and strong. *Composition III* 1955 (fig.23), a work that contradicts the richly sensuous paint of *Figure: Red and Black*, has a new type of austerity. Two lines of yellow paint, one broad, the other little more than a streak, burn their way through the dark background, emitting a glimmer of light. The edges of Rothko's forms have a glowing imprecision that is very similar. Another debt to Rothko is the way Scott divides the canvas horizontally, but whereas Rothko keeps resolutely to abstraction, Scott's composition keeps faith with the still life, reduced here to a tabletop and three barely identifiable objects.

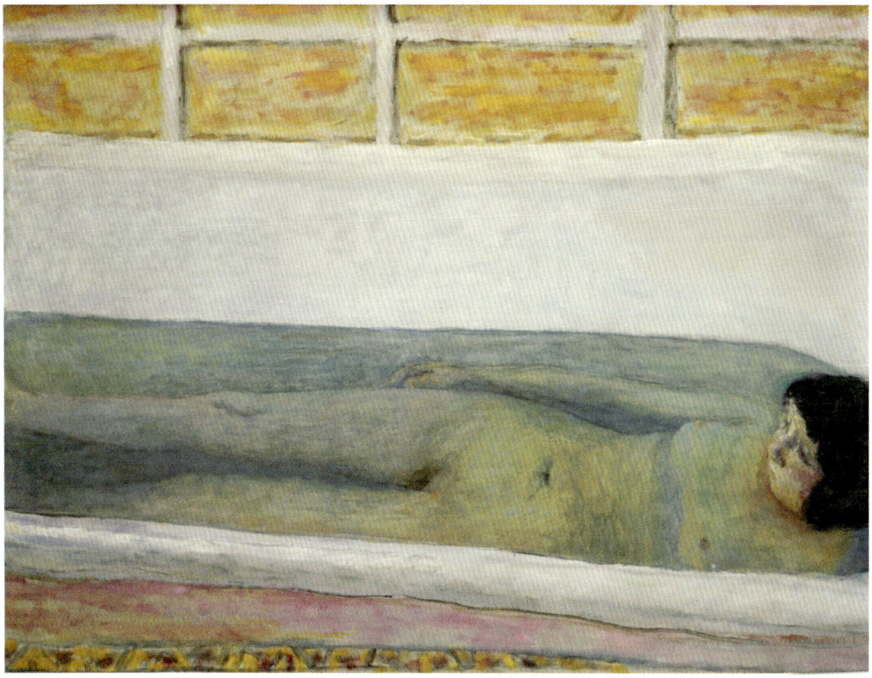

25
Pierre Bonnard
The Bath
1925
Oil on canvas
86 x 120.6
Tate. Presented by Lord Ivor Spencer Churchill through the Contemporary Art Society 1930

Just at the moment Scott was discovering the new American painting, the Americans were developing a taste for new European painting. In May 1955, for example, Scott was represented by four paintings in the exhibition *The New Decade: 22 European Painters and Sculptors*, which opened at the Museum of Modern Art, New York. The following year, in October, he had his first solo exhibition at Jackson's gallery, which, so Jackson told Scott, was much admired by Rothko.[24] One of the paintings Scott showed was the large *White Reclining Nude* 1956 (fig.24), a work Jackson kept on consignment and eventually sold to the Hirshhorn Museum in Washington, D.C. Based on Pierre Bonnard's *The Bath* (fig.25), it is a painting that broadcasts Scott's confident reaffirmation of his European roots. It was a work he knew particularly well, for not only did it hang in the Tate Gallery, he also kept a full-size copy of it in his London flat. The painter responsible for the copy was a former student at Corsham, Jo Gee, who, at Scott's request, exchanged it for one of Scott's own paintings. Gee recalled how Scott studied her copy of the Bonnard so closely 'that when he noticed a particular smudge on the breast or stomach of the model he would go off to the Tate to check if it was really there'.[25] Scott cannot have failed to notice how *The Bath*, with its softly defined horizontal divisions, had a close affinity with the paintings of Rothko.

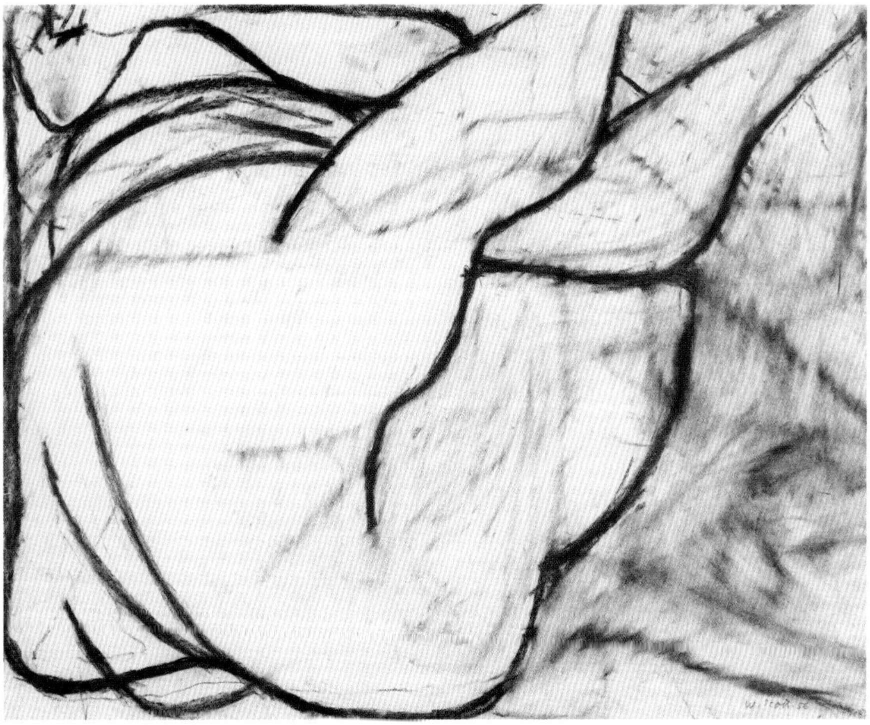

26

Nude

1956

Charcoal on paper

18 x 61

Private collection

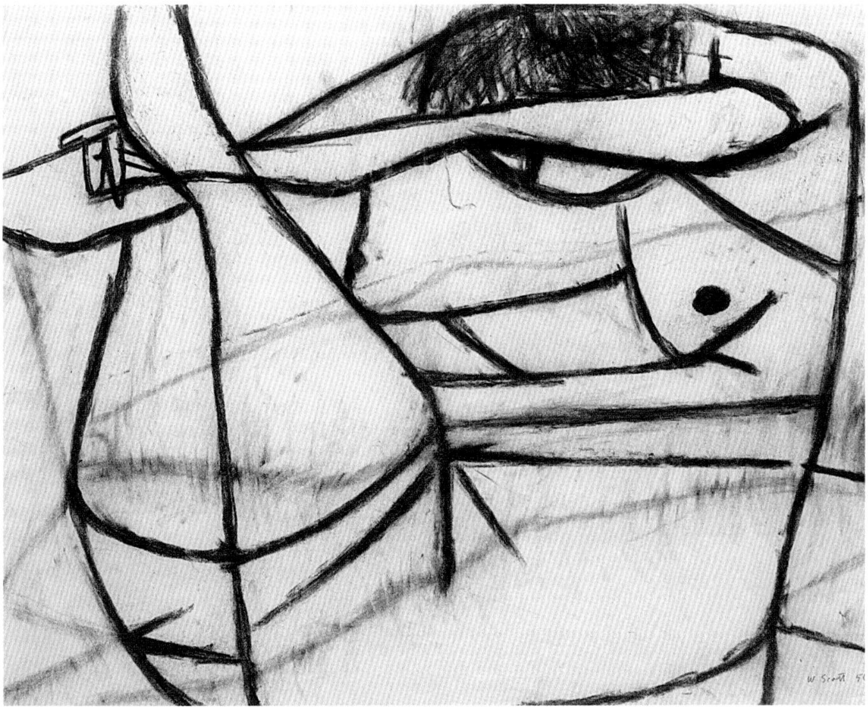

27

Nude Putting on Stockings

1956

Charcoal on paper

48.3 x 63.5

Tate. Presented by Jean-Yves Mock in memory of Mary and William Scott 2005

When Scott spoke about *White Reclining Nude* in a lecture he recorded for the British Council in 1959, he drew attention to the way the figure 'is stretched out like a landscape', a remark that takes us straight back to the earlier *Figure into Landscape*, which, when seen in the context of *White Reclining Nude*, reveals itself to be a highly abstracted rendering of the same nude stretched the length of her bathtub, the body a single line wandering unevenly across the canvas, her head a small neat square of black. As Scott explained in a rare statement published in the catalogue of *The New Decade* exhibition, 'it is in the act of making that the subject takes form, it is in the adding, stretching, taking away and searching for the right and exact statement that a tension is set up. I am horrified at the smart brush or any too easy method of gaining effect. I want to paint what I see but never immediately; there must be a time lapse, "a waiting time" for the visual experience to become involved with all other experience. That is why I paint from memory.'[26] Both *White Reclining Nude* and *Figure into Landscape* demonstrate how images stored away in an artist's visual memory will surface in ways that even the artist may find surprising.

Scott's remark that it is through the act of making that the subject takes shape is a reminder that in the mid-1950s – an intensely creative moment in his career – he began to use drawing in a completely new way. It was, he said, 'a kind of hastening up process'.[27] By this he meant that whereas he painted slowly he liked to draw rapidly without any corrections or erasures. Two charcoal figure studies of 1956, *Nude* (fig.26) and *Nude Putting on Stockings* (fig.27), look more like drawings done from memory than from life. The way in which the nude fills the entire sheet may owe something to the dramatic figure paintings and drawings Marie-Christine Treinen executed in the classrooms at Corsham; on the other hand, the emphasis on the buttocks, hips and thighs suggests lessons learned from Gustave Courbet, whose openly carnal paintings of the nude Scott knew at first hand (and copied). The subject apart, the drawings are particularly daring in the way they show the body, compressed and foreshortened to fit the size of the sheet (48 x 64 centimetres); at their simplest, they are rounded forms enclosed within a rectangle (the buttocks of *Nude* are as solidly balanced as one of Scott's kitchen bowls). The sensuality of both drawings is heightened by the close-up view: the bodies are shown within touching distance. The same year Scott painted *Reclining Nude* (fig.28), a large monochromatic figure, more monumental than *White Reclining Nude*, and more sculptural. It is not hard to visualise this weighty figure as a low relief carved out of some

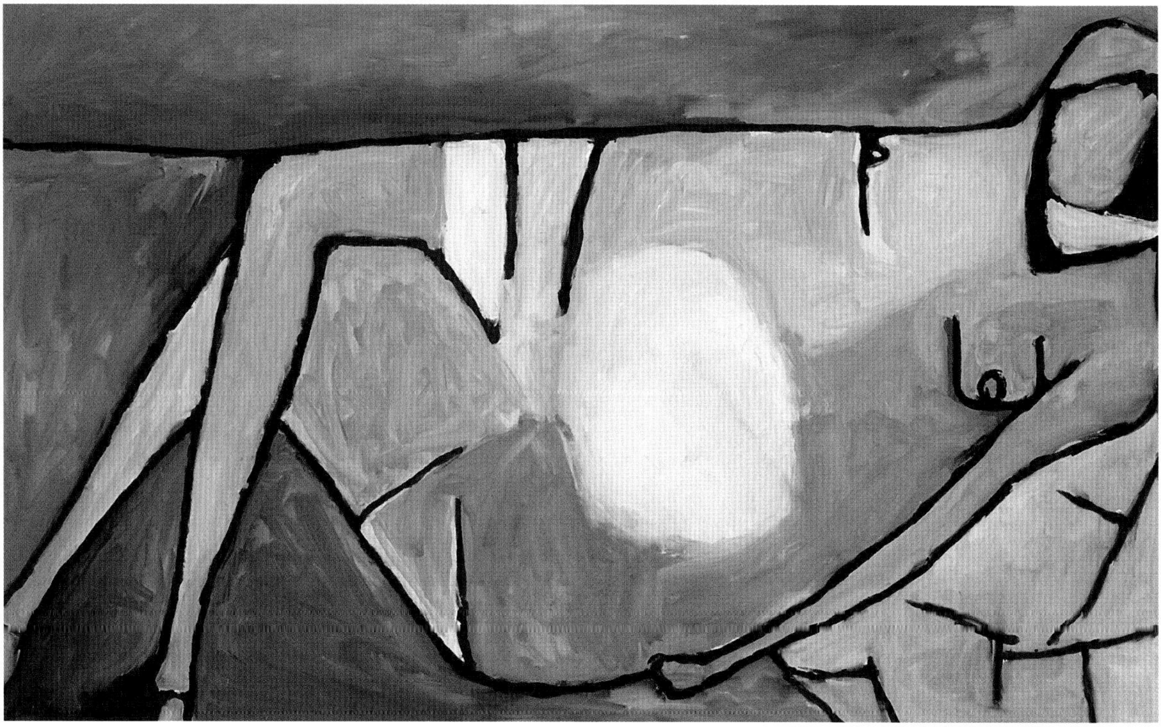

dark stone, and with good reason, for around this time Scott had taken up sculpture again. In August 1955 he had shown a large flat concrete female figure in the exhibition *New Sculptors and Painter-Sculptors* at the Institute of Contemporary Arts in London, and both *Reclining Nude* and *White Reclining Nude* were painted for an exhibition at the Hanover Gallery in September 1956 in which he also showed sculpture as well as drawings.

28
Reclining Nude
1956
Oil on canvas
92 x 152.5
Royal College of Art, London. Gift of E J Power

When Scott speaks of painting from memory he is not restricting himself to things seen in everyday life. Memories of familiar paintings play just as important a part in the retrieval process (the two drawings reproduced here are a mixture of memories of Courbet nudes and memories of studies made from life). Crucial to his way of working was what he calls the 'moment of transition'. By the mid-1940s, the Tate Gallery had acquired two important still lifes by Bonnard, *The Table* 1925 and *Coffee* 1915 (fig.29), paintings Scott knew as intimately as he knew *The Bath*. The difference between a work such as *Winter Still Life* (fig.30), painted by February 1956, and *Figure and Still Life* (fig.31) created later the same year, demonstrates the role Bonnard played in helping Scott find that moment of transition. *Winter Still Life*, a grand, severe painting, as icy

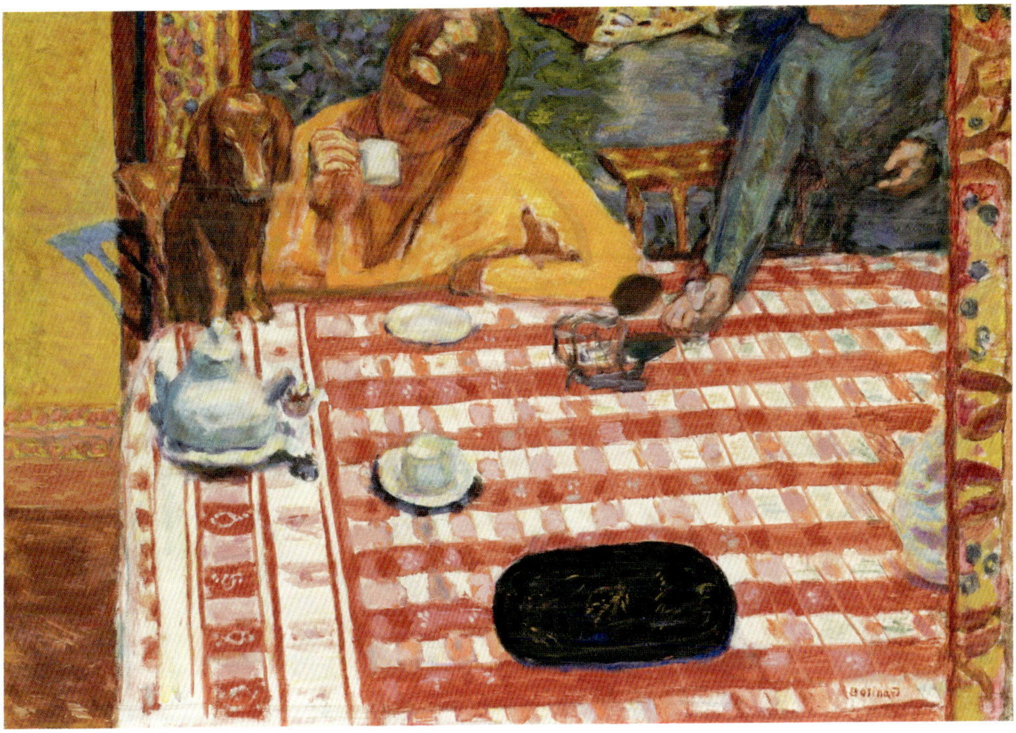

29
Pierre Bonnard
Coffee
1915
Oil on canvas
73 x 106.4
Tate. Presented by Sir Michael Sadler through the Art Fund 1941

cold as the subject demands, shows Scott's natural preference for simple geometrical divisions: the straight horizontal divide, the pots and pans aligned close to either the edges of the canvas or to the top edge of the table (the same anchoring device as seen in *Table Still Life* 1951), and the placing of the knife that hints at a strong vertical division between the frying pan on the left and the pans to the right. In *Figure and Still Life*, Scott lets go of the geometrical. The table, tilted upwards, occupies virtually the whole canvas. Its brilliant warm-orange surface is profusely crowded. Gone is the precise, almost geometrical ordering that governs the composition of *Winter Still Life*. Here the eye is not immediately directed but encouraged to wander randomly, to take its time. Bonnard's way of looking – to see everything and notice nothing – to break with the dogmatic presentation of traditional still life, came as an enormous release to a painter like Scott so thoroughly immersed in the history of the genre. One of Scott's reasons for pursuing the idea of the 'double image' had been to animate the composition through ambiguity (a figure that can be read as a landscape, for example): through Bonnard he found a new way in which to satisfy that desire to 'animate' (a word he often used). Two works painted the following year (1957) show how Scott understood and built

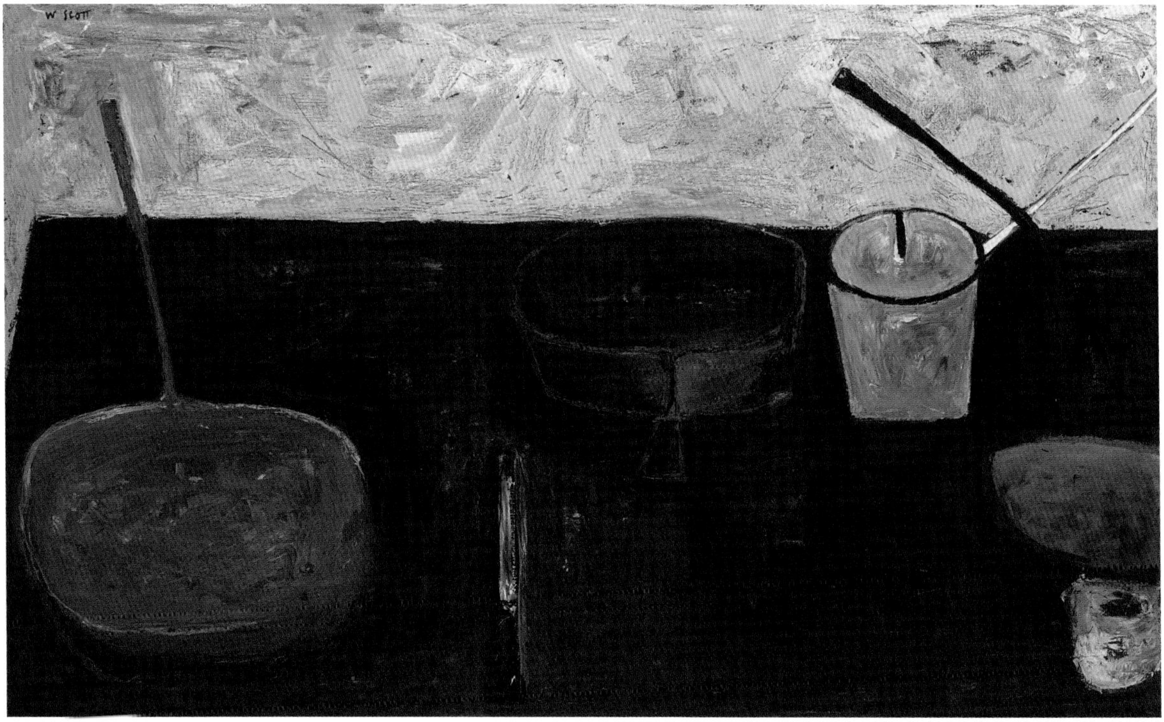

30
Winter Still Life
1956
Oil on canvas
91.4 x 152.4
Tate. Presented by the Contemporary Art Society 1957

on Bonnard's example. It was Scott's friend Patrick Heron who pointed out that Bonnard knew 'how to make a virtue of emptiness, how to keep a great expanse of the picture surface intensely meaningful without any resort to picture-filling incident'[28] (a lesson that underpins *Winter Still Life*). But, as Scott must have sensed, Bonnard also enjoyed making a virtue of excess. In *Large Still Life* 1957 (fig.32), the objects on the tabletop – now a bright clear blue – have to jostle for space as they nudge and bump their way across the wide expanse of blue (like boats at anchor). As Bonnard had noted in his diary some twenty years earlier, the principal subject for the painter was the surface, which, as he said, 'has its colour, its laws over and above those of objects'.[29] However casually arranged Bonnard's armoury of plates, baskets and bowls may appear, the whole is held in a sort of suspension by a precisely judged balance between solid and void. The way Scott arranges the objects around an open space placed at the centre in order to create a softer, more ambivalent division of the canvas than the more usual vertical or horizontal line, shows how carefully he had studied Bonnard's method. This hidden process of ordering is also seen in the way Scott punctuates the surface with accents of light and dark. Most of the bowls and pans are painted in white, very thickly

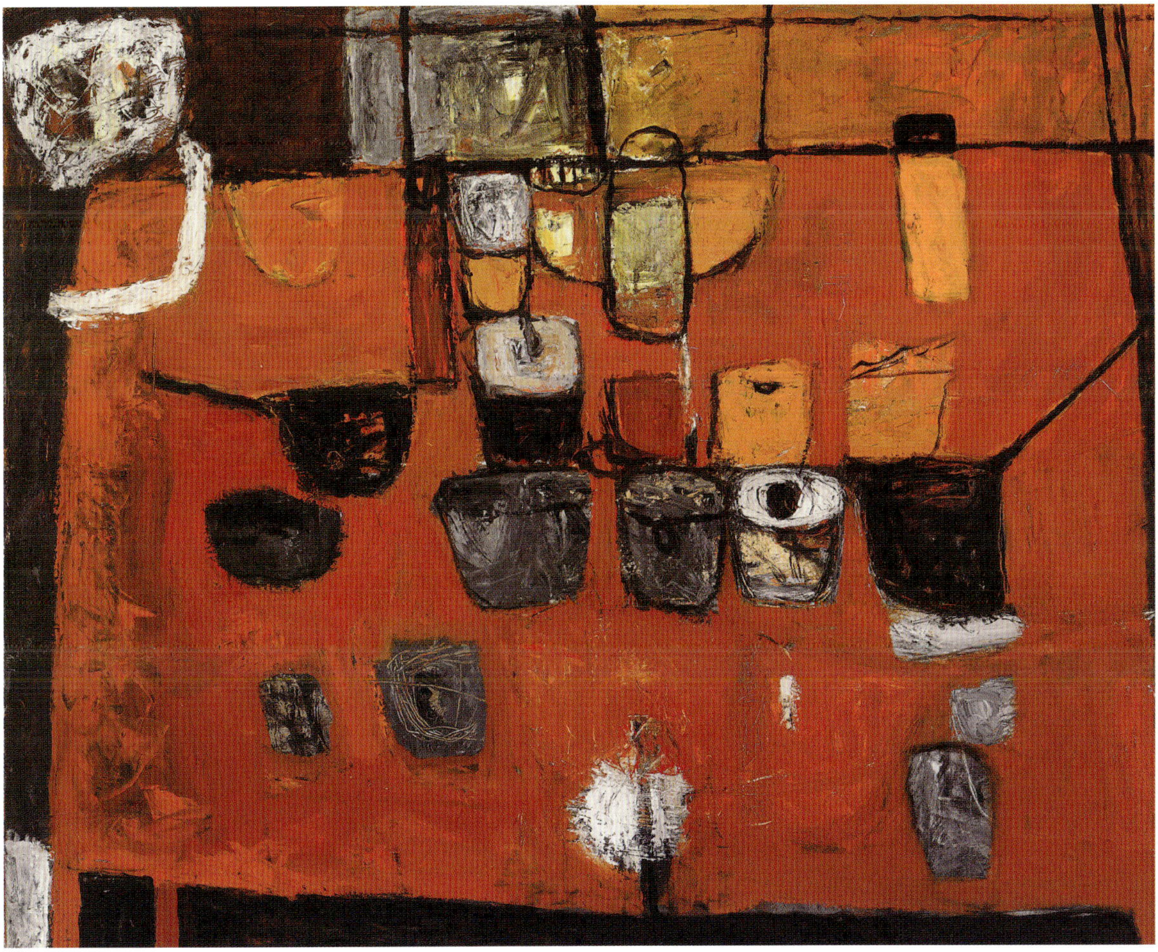

31

Figure and Still Life

1956

Oil on canvas

122 x 152

Private collection

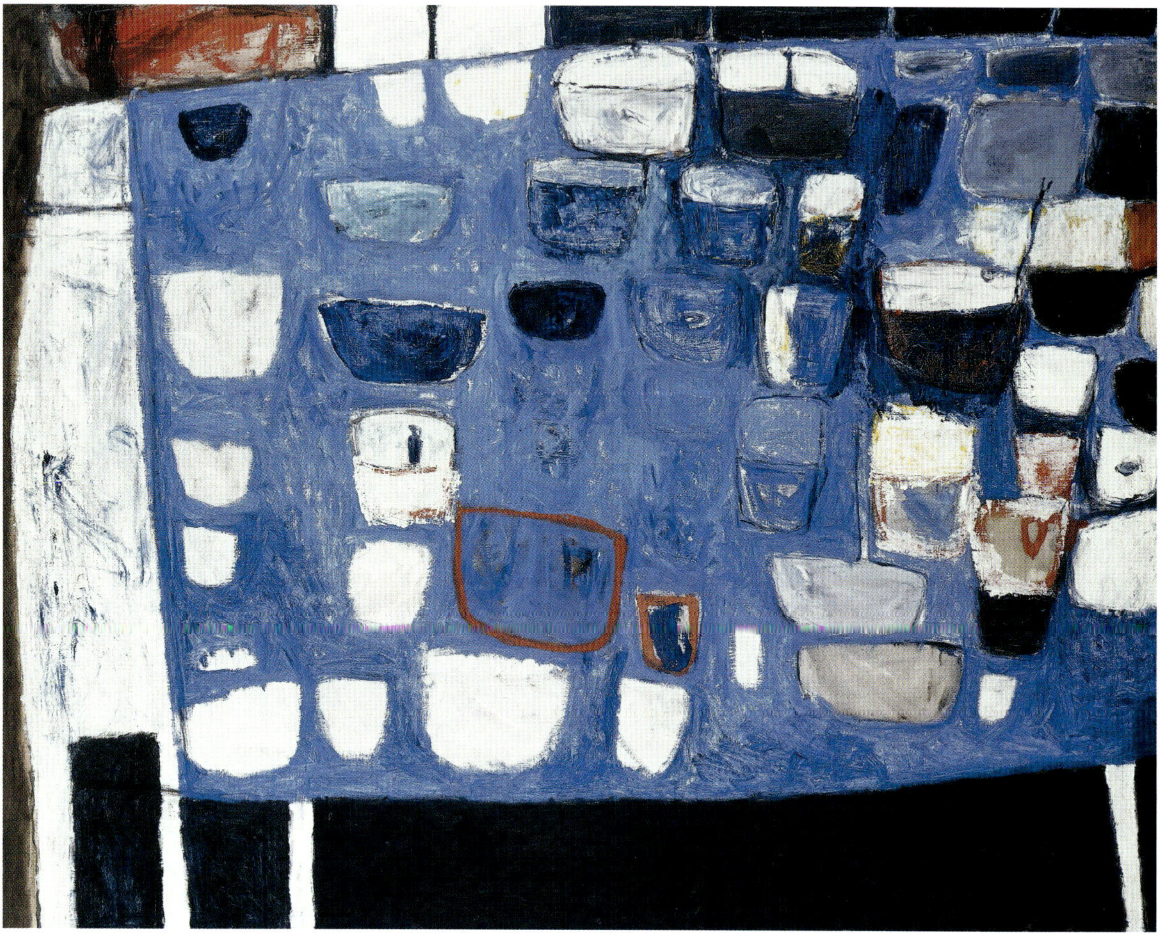

32

Large Still Life

1957

Oil on canvas

139 x 182

Private collection

applied, in striking contrast to the blue ground, while the composition as a whole is weighted down and secured by the few black-blue shapes deployed across the upper part of the table. Hidden too are the vestiges of objects that have been half obliterated by a coat of paint lightly skimmed over the surface. These 'ghosts' of discarded objects fill the spaces between their more solid counterparts like a piece of loose netting floating just beneath the surface. This unifying device suggests a comparison with the way Bonnard uses, with far greater emphasis, the red-and-white checked tablecloth in *Coffee*. The tablecloth turns into a web of colour that both separates and unifies the elements of the still life. A human presence half-hidden in the background is another element Scott borrows from Bonnard, but he does so in a way that is almost a parody of the original. The flat, ghostly face that protrudes above the left-hand edge of the table in *Figure and Still Life* is recognisably human, whereas in *Large Still Life* the figure standing by the table, to the left, and composed of two solid white blocks, is as inanimate an object as the table. It is hard to think of any other artist whose painting showed such a consummate understanding of Bonnard (Heron wrote about Bonnard with great insight, but as far as his own painting was concerned he looked more to Matisse). Scott would soon move on in other directions, but never again would another artist from the past offer him such valuable visual and moral support.

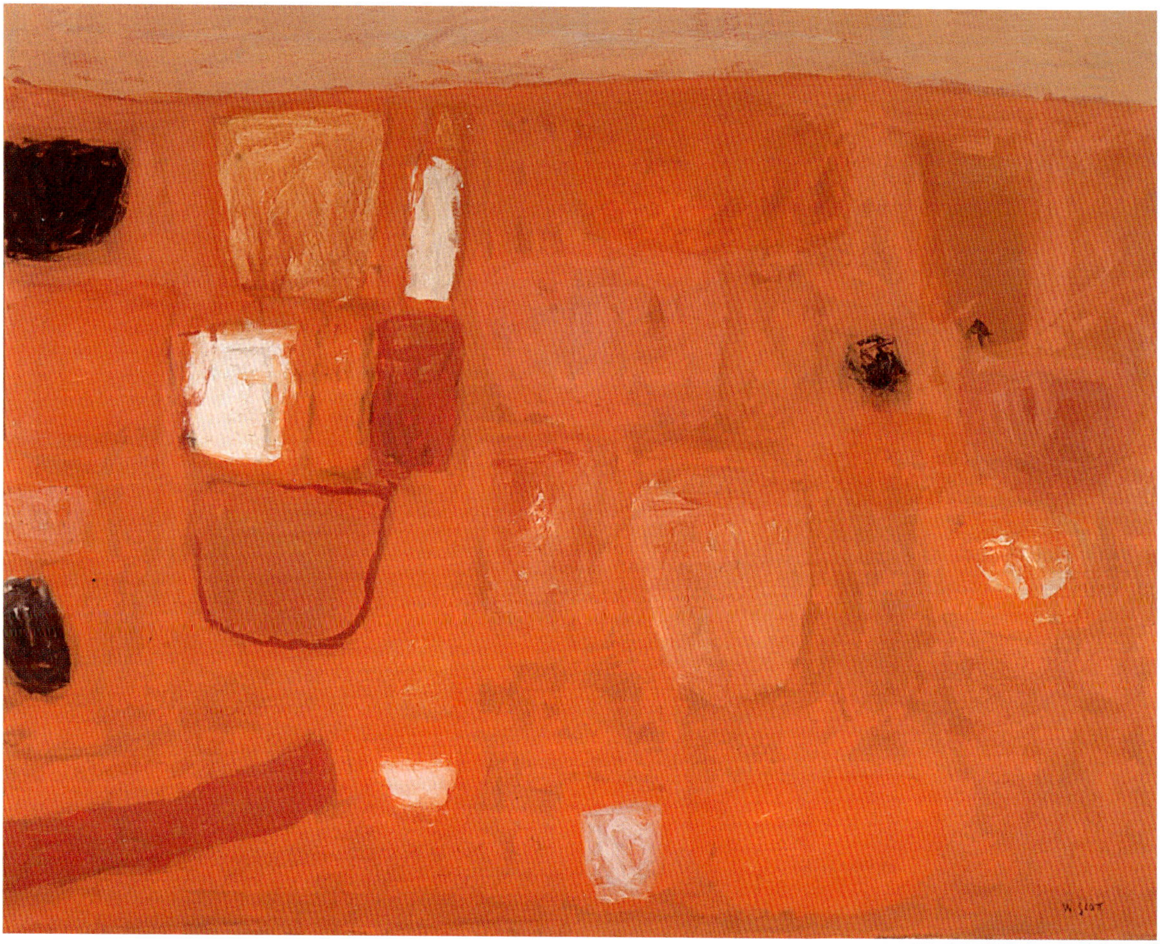

33

Orange and Red

1957

Oil on canvas

86.4 x 111.8

The Higgins Art Gallery

& Museum, Bedford

4 A LANGUAGE OF SIGNS

BY 1956, Scott was able to give up his teaching post at the Bath Academy of Art at Corsham in order to paint full time. Over the past few years, his reputation had been steadily growing both in England and abroad, and now the moment had come to concentrate exclusively on his work. The British Council, a hugely influential institution in those days, included his work in exhibitions they organised overseas, such as the British section of the second São Paulo Biennial in December 1953. As the art critic of *The Times* remarked in his review of *New Sculptors and Painter-Sculptors* at the Institute of Contemporary Arts in August 1955 (in which the artist had shown a sculpture), Scott's art had been 'recently blessed by one of those splendid and mysterious forward leaps that are the sure sign of a truly creative talent'.[30] He could now look to a more secure future, especially as he had now been taken on by two influential art dealers on opposite sides of the Atlantic: Erica Brausen, who ran the Hanover Gallery in London, and Martha Jackson in New York, who began to show Scott in October 1954, when she included twelve of his paintings in a joint exhibition with Barbara Hepworth and Francis Bacon.[31] Both Brausen and Jackson were powerful forces in the contemporary art world, energetically promoting the artists they took under their wing, and occasionally joining forces (although not without some fierce exchanges along the way). In June 1958, Scott was one of three artists chosen by the British Council to

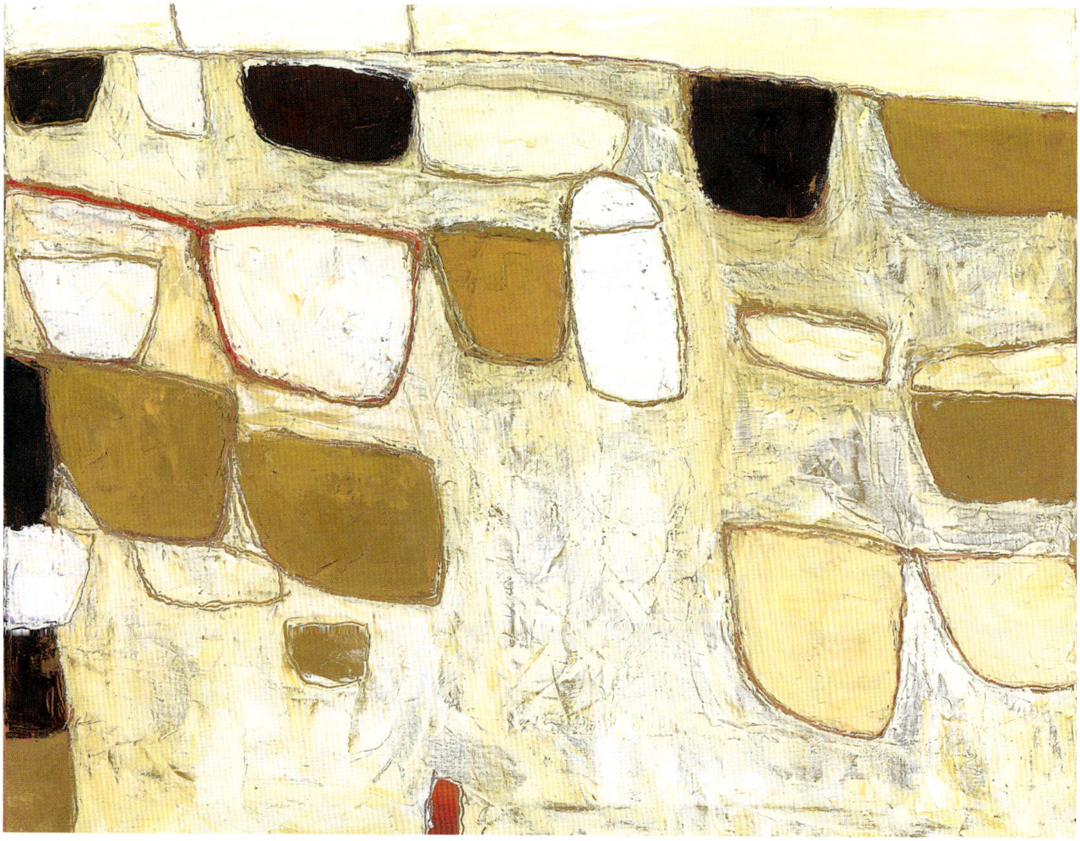

34
Ochre Still Life
1958
Oil on canvas
86.4 x 111.8
Tate. Purchased 1962

represent Britain at the Venice Biennale, an accolade that helped secure his position as an artist of international standing.

Scott's growing confidence in the mid-1950s was fuelled in part by a reaction against the sort of hard-edged abstract art he regarded as 'too smartly done, too beautifully done, too tasteful, too perfect ... so well done one loses a sense of humanity about it'. His belief in 'the beauty of the thing badly done'[32] is expressed in the way he piles up layer after layer of different textures: fat glossy paint, thin paint, paint scraped back almost to bare canvas, lines scrawled and scratched into the surface next to lines made by squeezing paint straight from the tube. His disregard for perfection also allowed him to stay nearer to the messy vitality of life, to keep hold of the struggle and tension that had gone into the making of a composition. Almost all of his paintings of this period, however abstract they may appear, are tied to reality by the inclusion of a horizon. In *Orange and Red* 1957 (fig.33), the still life gradually loses all definition: the edge of the table meanders across the top of the canvas

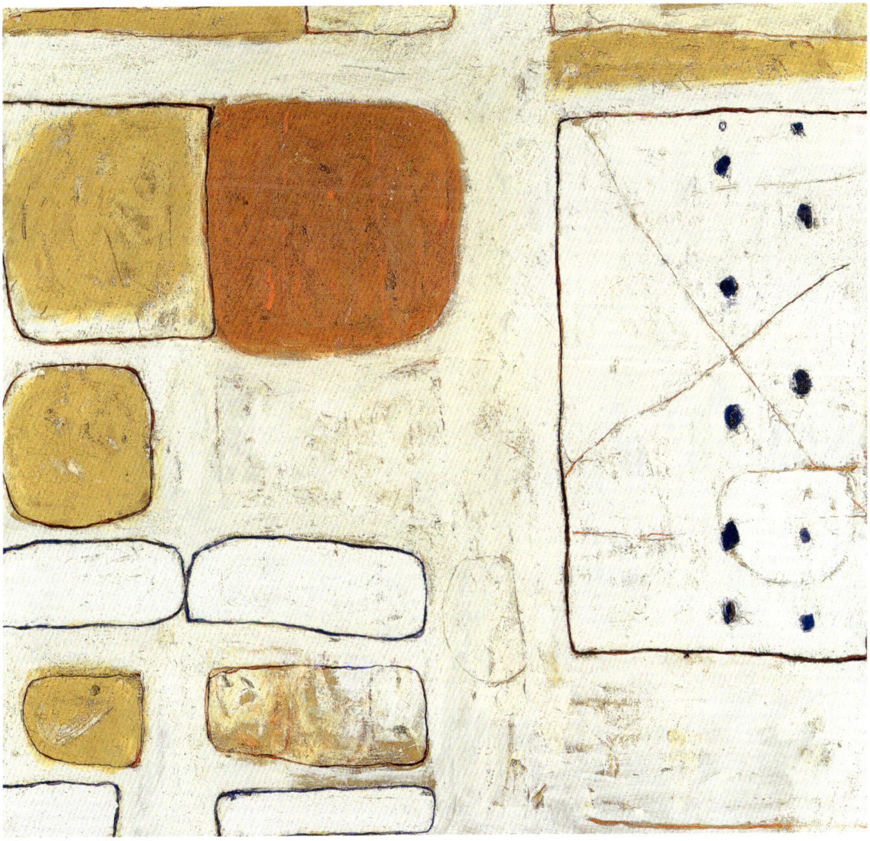

35
White, Sand and Ochre
1960–1
Oil on canvas
160 x 172.7
Tate. Purchased 1961

like a distant hill in a landscape, and the objects, subjected to the blaze of orange, are reduced to molten vestiges of the bowls and pans they once were. The still life, densely packed as in *Figure and Still Life*, has now begun to drift, the various elements anchored only by the two black forms on the left. That anchoring device is used again in *Ochre Still Life* 1958 (fig.34), where five black forms of varying sizes are posted around two sides of the canvas as though to contain the surface ebb and flow. This is a prelude to the next step in which the objects lose their identity altogether.

One of Scott's earliest memories of his childhood in Greenock was playing hopscotch, a street game popular with the local children: 'In the summer we played in the streets in our bare feet, the pavement and walls covered in chalk patterns on which we jumped and skipped.' The rough marks made by white chalk on an abrasive surface is a motif that runs through Scott's work. In his charcoal drawings, for instance, the lines made with a stick of black charcoal leave the same furred outline on the white paper as

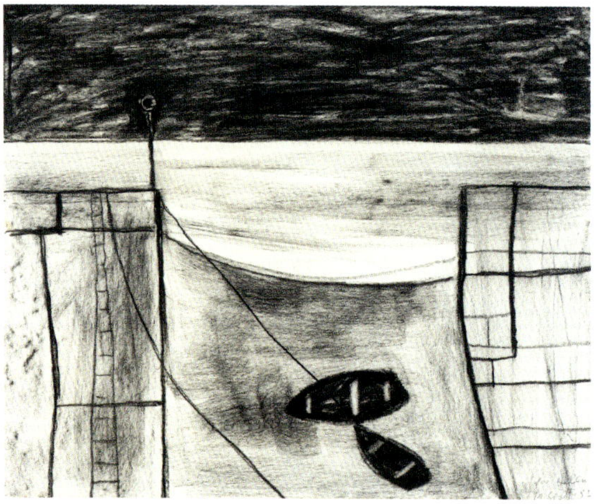

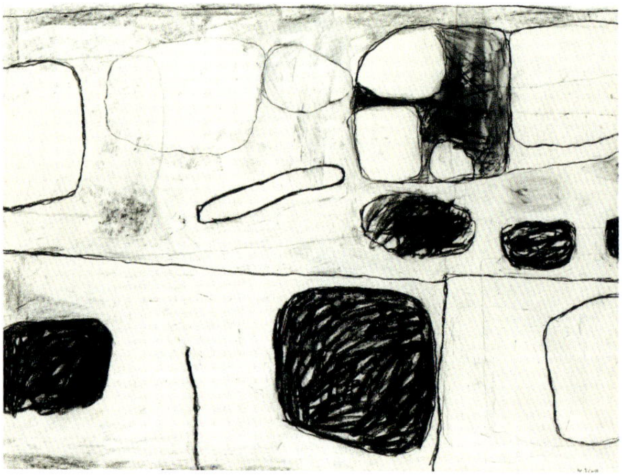

36
Study for Cornish Harbour
1951
Charcoal on paper,
Approx. 32 x 39.4
Private collection

37
Drawing for a Painting
1953
Charcoal on paper
20.3 x 26
Private collection

white chalk does on a pavement or a wall. Or, as in the oil paintings, faint outlines of shapes that have been painted over hover beneath the surface like half-erased chalk marks left by childrens' games. Scott may well have thought back to his childhood when, in the summer of 1955, returning from a family holiday on the Catalan coast, he visited Lascaux in south-western France to see the palaeolithic cave paintings. As he later said, 'the experience of seeing some of the most remarkable paintings ever made, had I think, a profound impression on my future work'.[33] The paintings Scott would have seen (in the days when visitors could still enter the caves) were not only the celebrated depictions of animals, but also abstract imagery composed of dots and lines, as well as geometric shapes such as triangles, circles and pentagons. *White, Sand and Ochre* 1960–1 (fig.35) and *Forms on White* 1960 (fig.40) are both compositions in which the white background has the scumbled look of a stone wall worn away by the centuries. Over this surface, Scott draws (using a fine paintbrush) lines and dots, circles and brick-shaped forms, laid out like ancient pictographs whose patterns offer some elusive meaning like the enigmatic signs at Lascaux. The two paintings work as a pair: the dimensions of each canvas, 160 x 173 centimetres, make them appear slightly wider than they are high, proportions that are similar to those of a typical Scott tabletop in, for example, *Figure and*

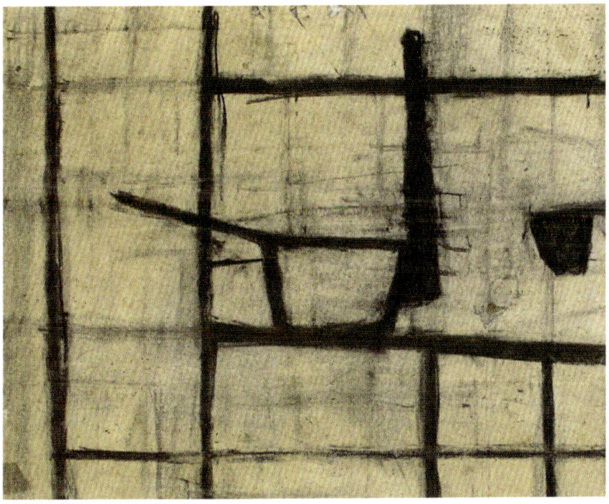

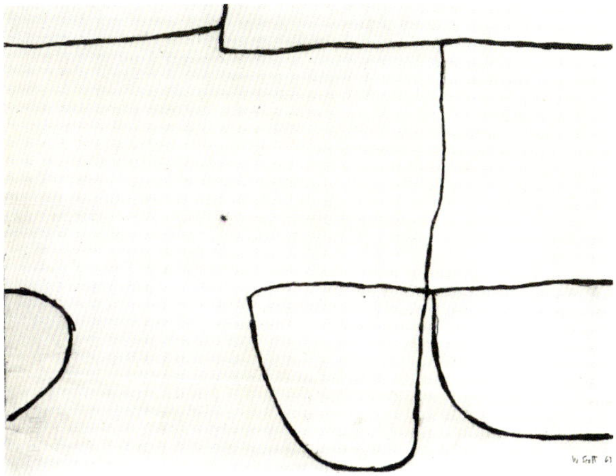

38
Strata
1958
Charcoal on paper
56 x 76
Private collection

39
Forms Integrating 1
1963
Charcoal on paper
48 x 65
Private collection

Still Life. The composition in both *White, Sand and Ochre* and *Forms on White* is almost identical, with the exception of the clearly separated circle and square in *Forms on White*, a pairing that dissolves under the weight of colour in the other painting. Making two different versions of the same painting was a habit that served several purposes. On a practical level, if Scott thought a painting was particularly successful, a second version allowed him to exhibit it both in New York with Jackson and in London with Brausen. On a painterly level, it allowed him to play around with light and dark versions, experimenting with the way density and balance can be altered through colour. The strong patches of ochre and sand in *White, Sand and Ochre* are balanced by nothing more assertive than the pale blue of the tablet form on the right, a reminder of how consistently Scott relied on his instinct as a tonal painter. The Tate Gallery bought *White, Sand and Ochre* soon after it was painted and, as was customary, wrote to the artist requesting information about its genesis. Scott, usually reluctant to respond to direct questions about his painting, came up with a typically succinct answer: 'A source of inspiration towards its making may be my strong liking for Egyptian painted art.'[34] Even without that clue it is easy to see how the limestone reliefs Scott looked at on his many visits to the Egyptian rooms at the British Museum would have appealed to his liking for rough textures

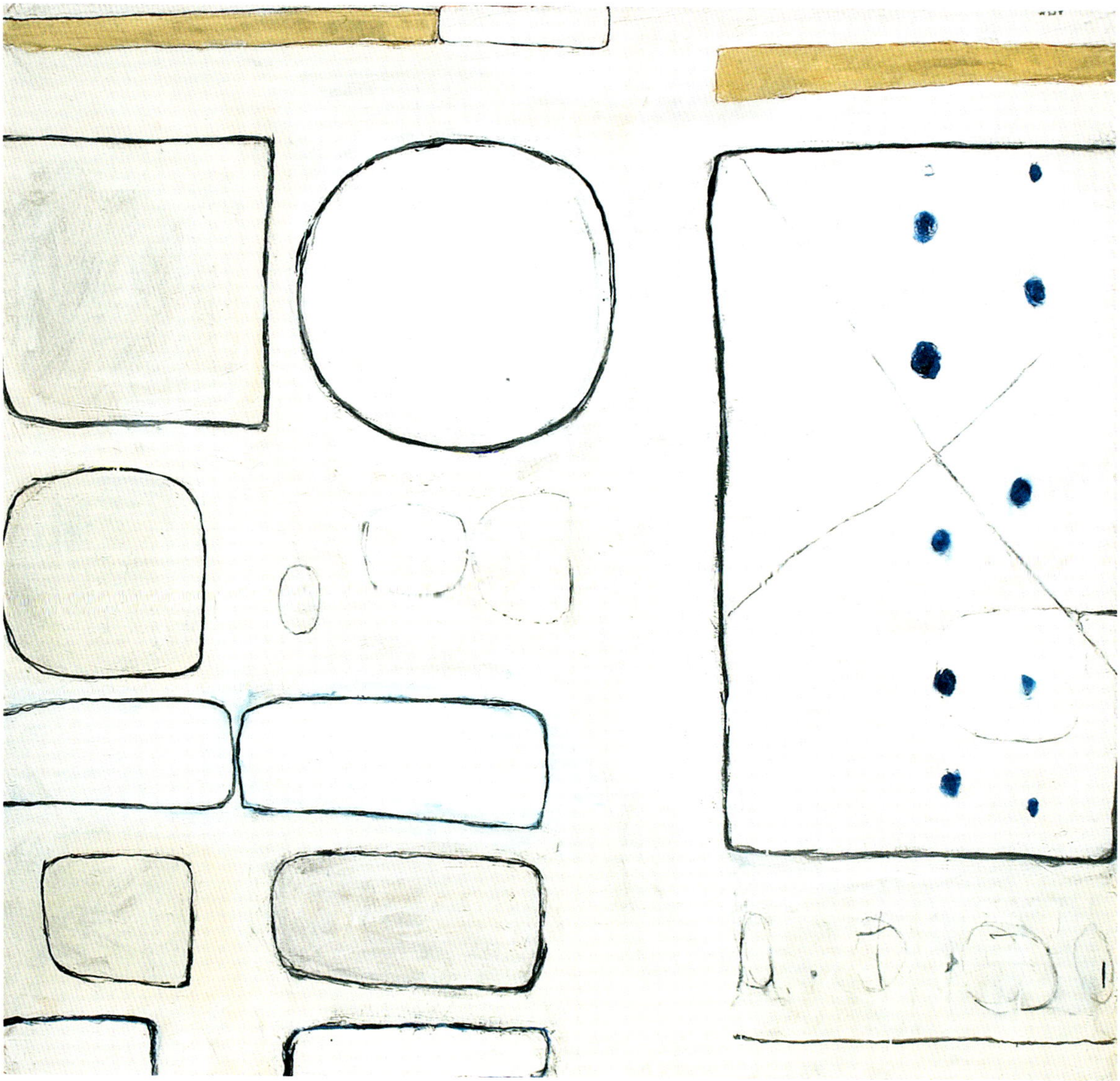

40

Forms On White

1961

Oil on canvas

160 x 173

Hirshhorn Museum and Sculpture Garden, Smithsonian Institution,

The Martha Jackson Memorial Collection: Gift of Mr and Mrs David K Anderson, 1980

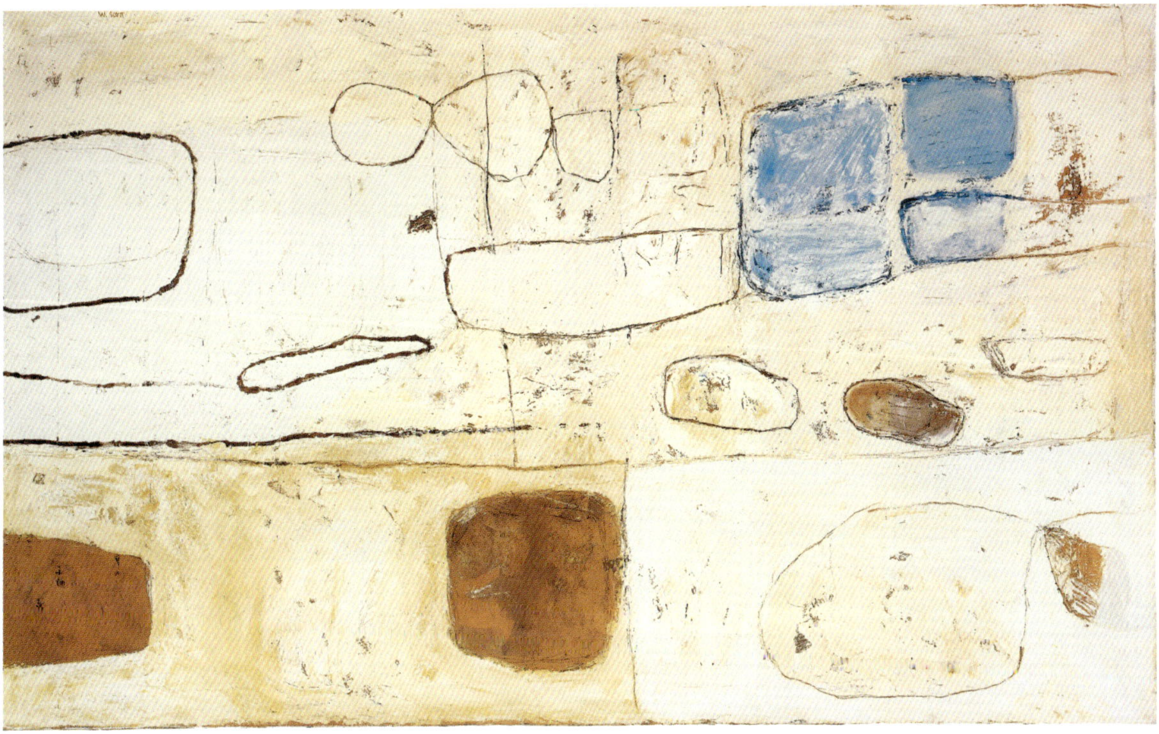

41
Egyptian Memory
1958
Oil on canvas
111.8 x 182.9
Private collection

and rich earthy colours. *Egyptian Memory* 1958 (fig.41), for example, is a work that not only reveals its source through the title, but through its tabletlike proportions. Areas of paint in *White, Sand and Ochre* are mixed with sand, creating heavy lumps of impasto, some of which appear to be built up around staples fired into the canvas. This gives the lines drawn on the surface the appearance of being incised into the paint. The free-floating forms in *Egyptian Memory* have the look of signs scratched into a hard surface. These casually drawn, but carefully controlled shapes, can also be seen as objects carried along by water, the landscape in the title suggesting the flow of the River Nile. As in *Table Still Life* and *Large Still Life*, floating is a persistent, if hidden theme. In the summer of 1962, a major exhibition of Egyptian art opened at the Royal Academy of Arts, London,[35] an event that may have encouraged Scott to paint two more 'Egyptian' works, *Nile Valley: Red and White* (fig.42), which was completed by August that year, and *Nile Valley: Morning* (fig.43). Unlike the earthy colours of *White, Sand and Ochre* and the more limpid palette of *Egyptian Memory*, the accents of red and orange laid against a hazy white powerfully convey the blazing heat, the arid earth, and the blinding light of the Nile Valley.[36]

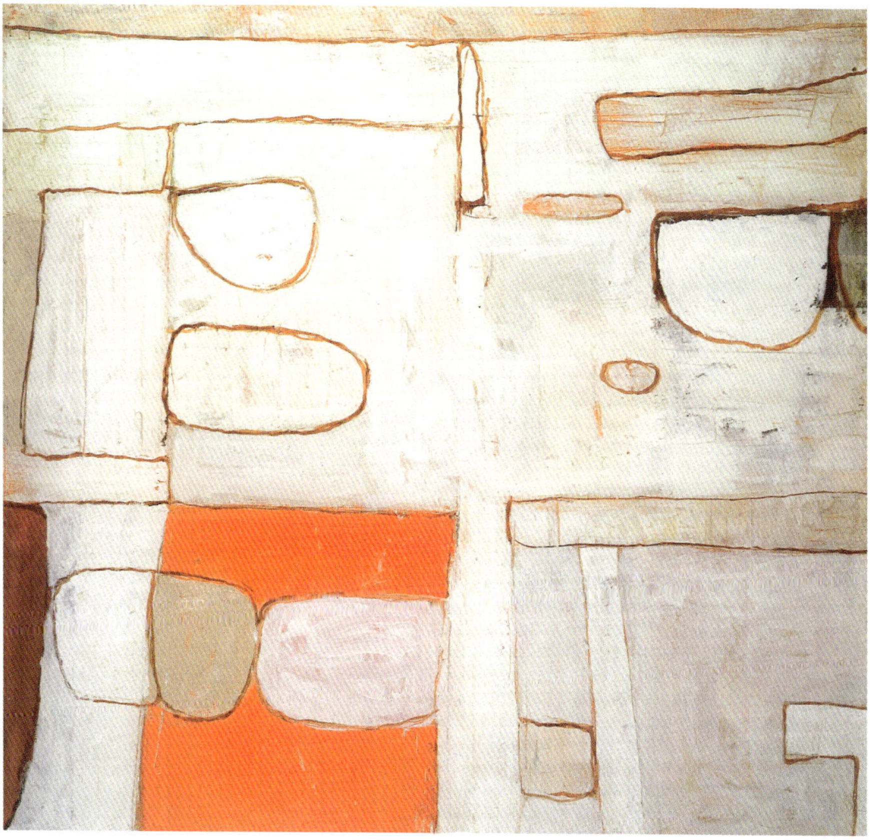

42
Nile Valley: Red and White
1962
Oil on canvas
160 x 173
Private collection

Many of the works Scott painted from the mid-1950s to the early 1960s carry within them memories of his visit to New York in August 1953. When he showed *Ocean* (fig.44) at his solo exhibition at the Hanover Gallery in May 1961, its kinship with the paintings of Rothko did not go unnoticed. The upright format and the division of the canvas into fields of colour separated by two thin streaks of white would naturally invite a comparison with the American artist, although John Russell (who wrote the catalogue introduction) was quick to point out that Scott's own personality had the last word, 'with graffiti-like markings to relate the picture to the life of the street and the wraiths of Scott's *batterie de cuisine* to remind us that we are, after all, three thousand miles away from New York'.[37] The title refers directly to the ocean mass separating the British Isles from the vastness of the American continent, but also implicit in that title is the idea that a stretch of water links as much as it divides. In August 1959, Rothko and his family spent the summer touring Europe, and in mid-August they went to stay with the Scotts in their house in Somerset. Before Rothko

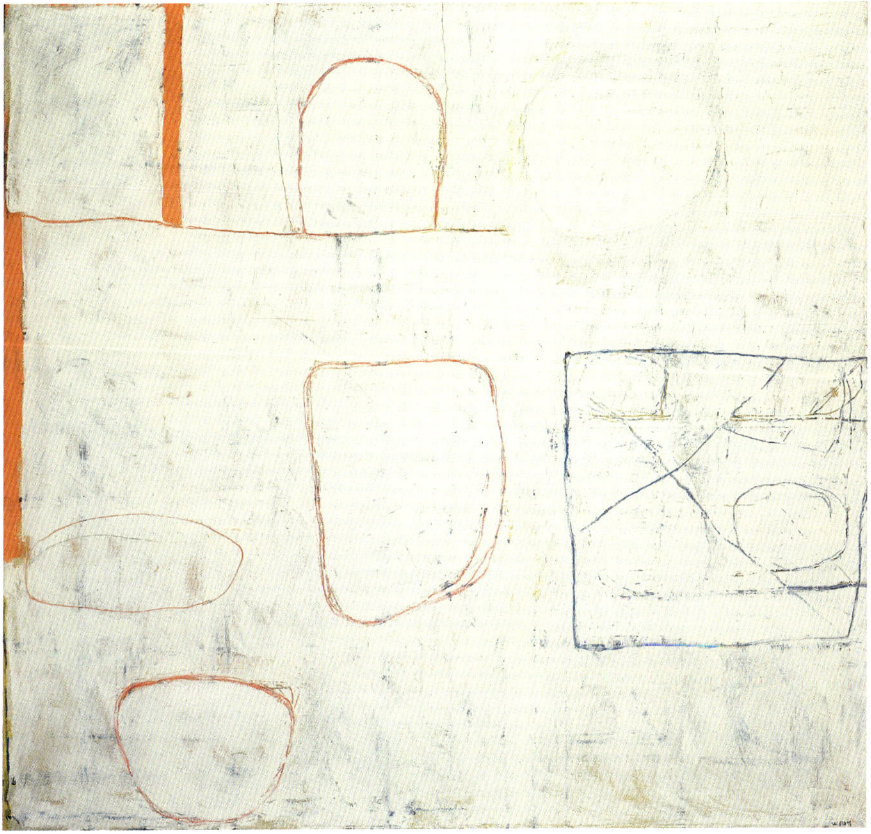

43
Nile Valley: Morning
1962
Oil on canvas
160 x 173
Albright-Knox Art Gallery, Buffalo, New York. Gift of Martha Jackson to the Room of Contemporary Art, 1967

left for Europe, he was on the point of completing his murals for The Four Seasons restaurant in the Seagram Building in New York, a series of glowing austere canvases, nine of which he would eventually present to the Tate Gallery. If there is a connection between *Ocean* and Rothko, it is more likely to have come out of this meeting in England than their first encounter in New York exactly six years earlier. As a young man, Rothko had read Nietzsche's *Birth of Tragedy* with great attention, and a passage in that famous essay was quoted by Peter Selz, curator of painting and sculpture at the Museum of Modern Art, New York, in his catalogue introduction to the retrospective Rothko exhibition that travelled to London in October 1961.[38] The passage reads: 'There is need for a whole world of torment in order for the individual to produce the redemptive vision and to sit quietly in his rocking row-boat in mid-sea, absorbed in contemplation.'[39] It is too speculative to suggest that this particular passage might have come up in the conversations the two painters had enjoyed in the summer of 1959 (although they certainly shared a love of literature),

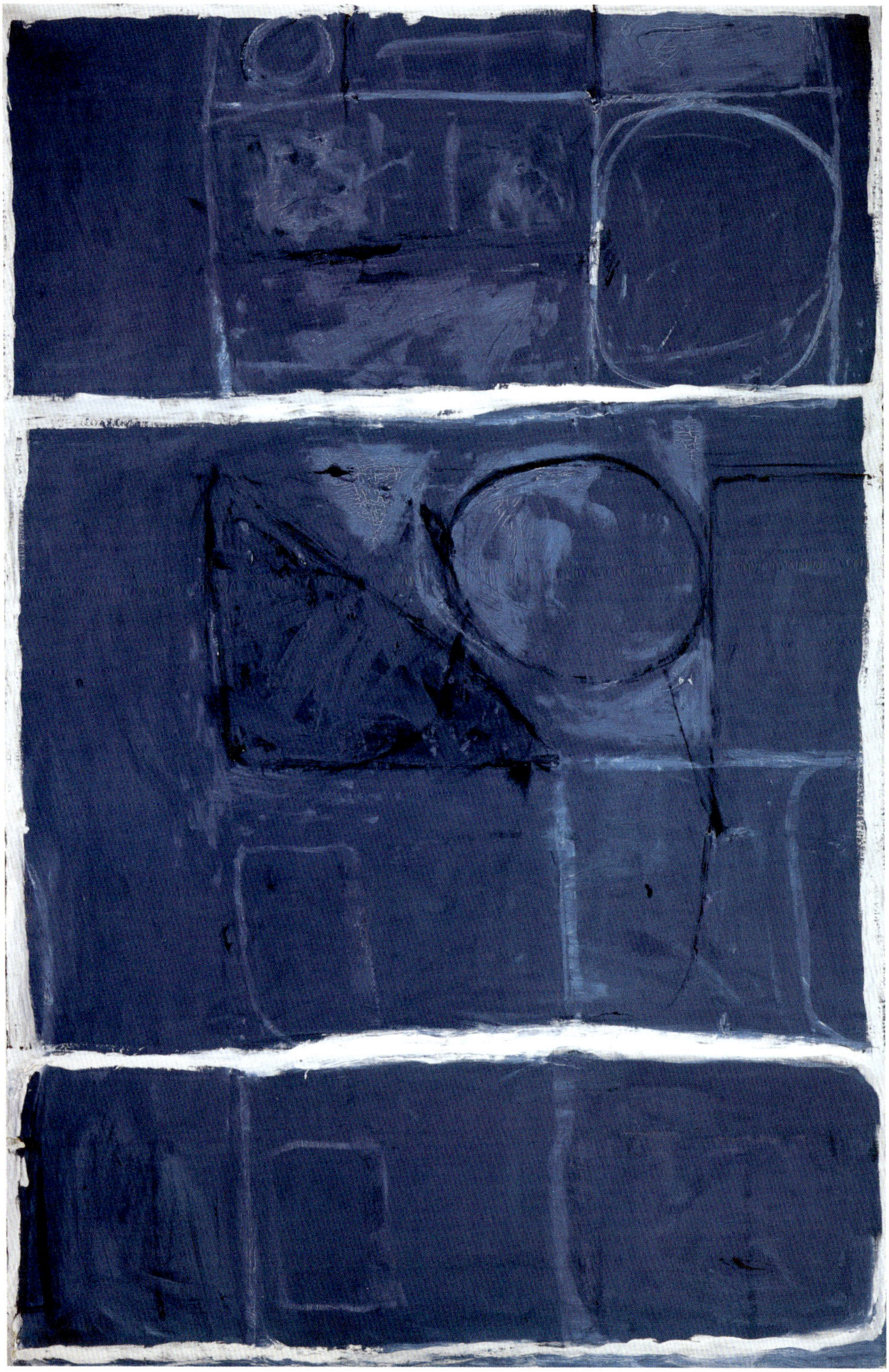

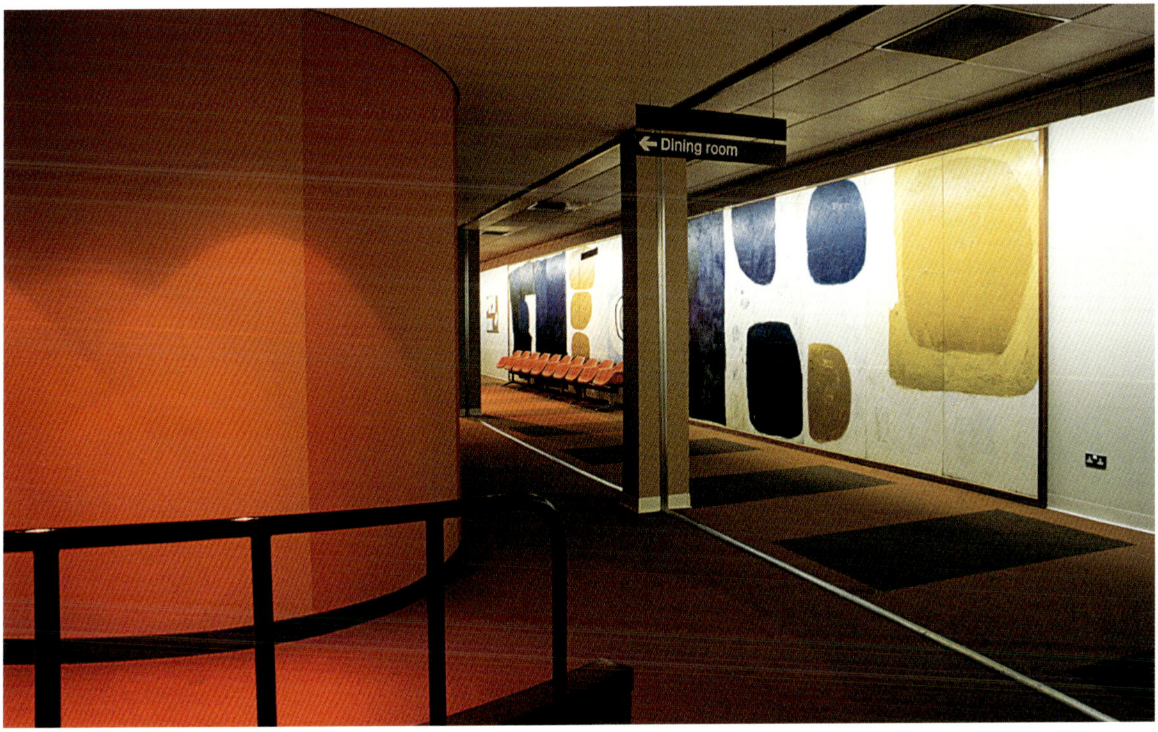

45
Installation view of William Scott's mural at Altnagelvin Hospital, Londonderry

but the image of the 'rocking row-boat in mid-sea' is one that Scott, had he known it, would surely have understood and even recognised its relevance to his own painting. The tabletop still lifes of the mid-1950s, which can also be read as harbours sheltering boats at anchor, are as much paintings of reflection and contemplation as they are of still life. Looking at the veiled blue surface of *Ocean*, and the suggestion it carries of a hidden world beneath, it is tempting to see the painting as a conscious response to the redemptive nature of Rothko's art, and to his deeply held belief in 'the simple expression of the complex thought'.[40]

'Stern dignity and absolute honesty merge in an almost religious impact', wrote one critic after seeing *Ocean*.[41] Those words, written in the context of that painting, are just as relevant to a mural commission that occupied Scott between September 1958 and September 1961. Murals were the one subject that Scott and Rothko are known to have discussed during the short time they spent together in August 1959. By that stage Scott had only just started work on an ambitious mural commissioned by the architectural firm Yorke Rosenberg and Mardall for the entrance hall of Altnagelvin Hospital in Londonderry, Northern Ireland (figs.45–6). The scale of the commission was

44
Ocean
1960 or 1961
Oil on canvas
183.5 x 122.4
Sir Alan and Lady Bowness

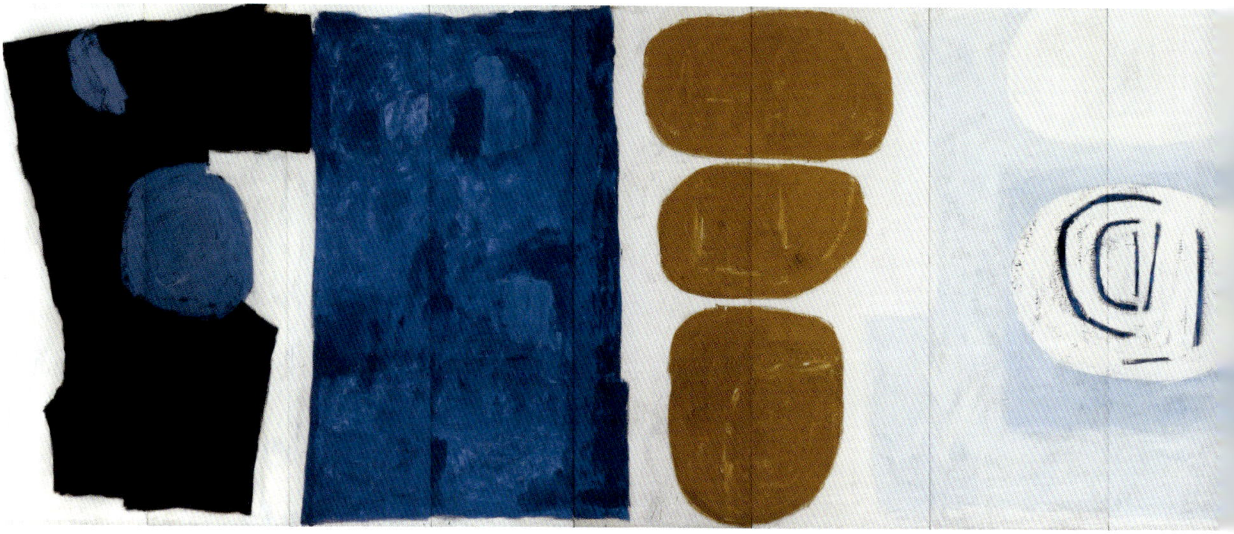

46
Altnagelvin Mural
1959–62
Oil on plywood
274.3 x 1,371.6
Altnagelvin Hospital, Londonderry

something entirely new for Scott, and it is hardly surprising that it took him nearly a year even to figure out how to start. Eugene Rosenberg, the senior partner in the firm, turned out to be the best possible ally when it came to dealing with the more conservative elements in the hospital administration. Scott let it be known that he wanted to do a mural that was in keeping with Ireland, even with the Londonderry site itself, and he sought the help of Eric Jones, the secretary of the hospital. He must have been startled at what the hospital official came up with. Under the heading 'Let There Be Light', Jones had taken as his theme 'man's journey to enlightenment, law, order, justice and mercy', a journey he interpreted as an epic history of Londonderry told through a cast of saints and soldiers, colonels and bishops, farmers and tradesmen, all to be pictured against a landscape of fields, farms, factories and churches.[42] How Scott handled this daunting suggestion is not known, but Jones's scenario, however comically overblown it may seem now, gives a sobering idea of local expectations. As it happened, Scott stayed with the idea of Irish history, but approached it through his research into ancient Celtic art rather than through Jones's pictorial history books. The dozens of notes and sketches he made for the mural show his ideas progressing from the imagery of ancient Ireland, such as crosses, rounded towers and intricate symbolic patterns, to the elemental forces of earth, air, water and fire. Right from the beginning, he and Rosenberg had agreed that the mural should be abstract, but Scott wanted the abstract to be informed not by any literal meaning, but by suggestion, by the sort of mysterious meanings that lie buried for centuries in ancient signs and pictographs.

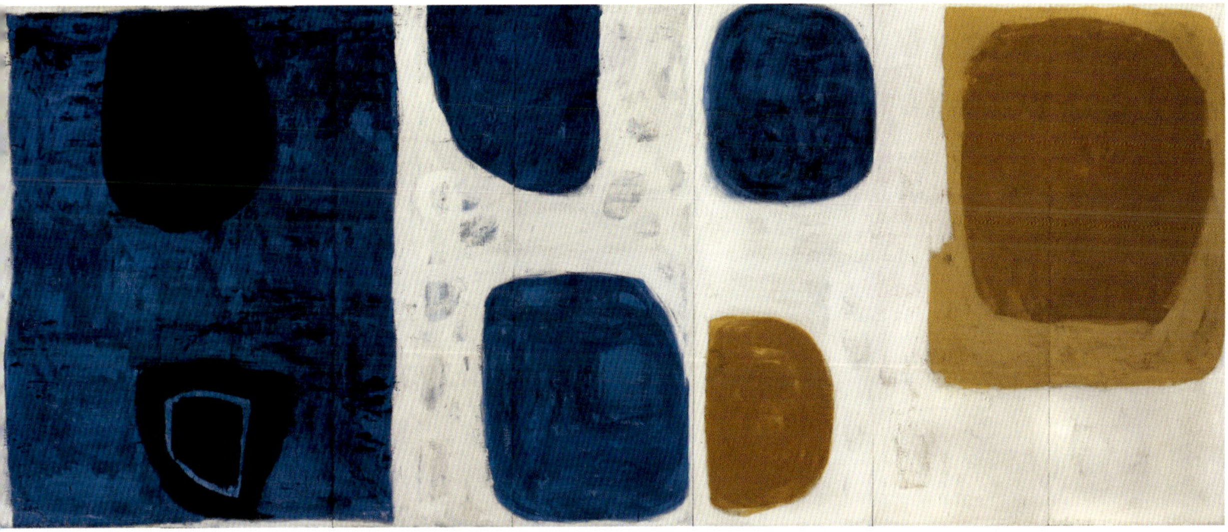

Scott worked on the mural in his studio in Hallatrow, where, for lack of space, he had to spread the panels over three walls of one room and two walls in an adjoining room (which Mary Scott had used as her sculpture studio). Shuttling between the two spaces, he would carry cut-out pieces of paper and pin them to the plywood panels to try out what he called 'my shapes'. Little is known about the progress of the mural, but it evidently went through several stages, beginning with Scott working on each of the fifteen panels separately before deciding to divide them into pairs, leaving one to stand alone. At one stage, he was working with a range of bright oranges, salmon pinks, light yellows and blues (colours that were found underneath when the mural was restored in 2010). The darker, more austere colours of the final version, dark blues deepened in places by black, ochres, light cerulean blue and blue-whites, are colours that suggest the raw elements of an island landscape; earth, air and water. Recent American painting may have given Scott the confidence to take on the scale of these panels, but it was the ancient art of Ireland that helped him find the visual language. The shell-like motif in the centre of the mural is closely related to the prehistoric carvings in the passage graves and stone circles found all over Northern Ireland, while the heavy texturing of the paint in the other panels recall the ancient weathering of prehistoric monoliths. Even so, the grand gestural forms that fill these panels owed more to American painting than any other painting being produced in this country. Scott had been 'overwhelmed', as he put it by the scale and the directness of the work he had seen in 1953 when he visited New York. In February 1959, when he had barely started work on the panels, he had a fresh encounter with the Abstract Expressionists when the exhibition *The New American Painting*, organised by Alfred Barr, opened at the Tate Gallery. The grand sweep of the black-and-white paintings of Franz Kline and Robert Motherwell must have inspired Scott with their astonishing monumentality. Their works, as Barr had observed at the time, were 'as big as mural paintings'.[43]

In November 1961, Scott's mural was shown at the Tate Gallery before being installed at Altnagelvin. When it was unveiled at the hospital a few months later, before a large invited audience, the response was one of horrified silence. According to Mary Scott, who had been asked to pull the cord at the opening ceremony, 'People stared, stunned and silent. There was no sound at all. Within less than twenty minutes the room was empty.'

Nile Valley: Red and White
1962 (detail of fig.42)

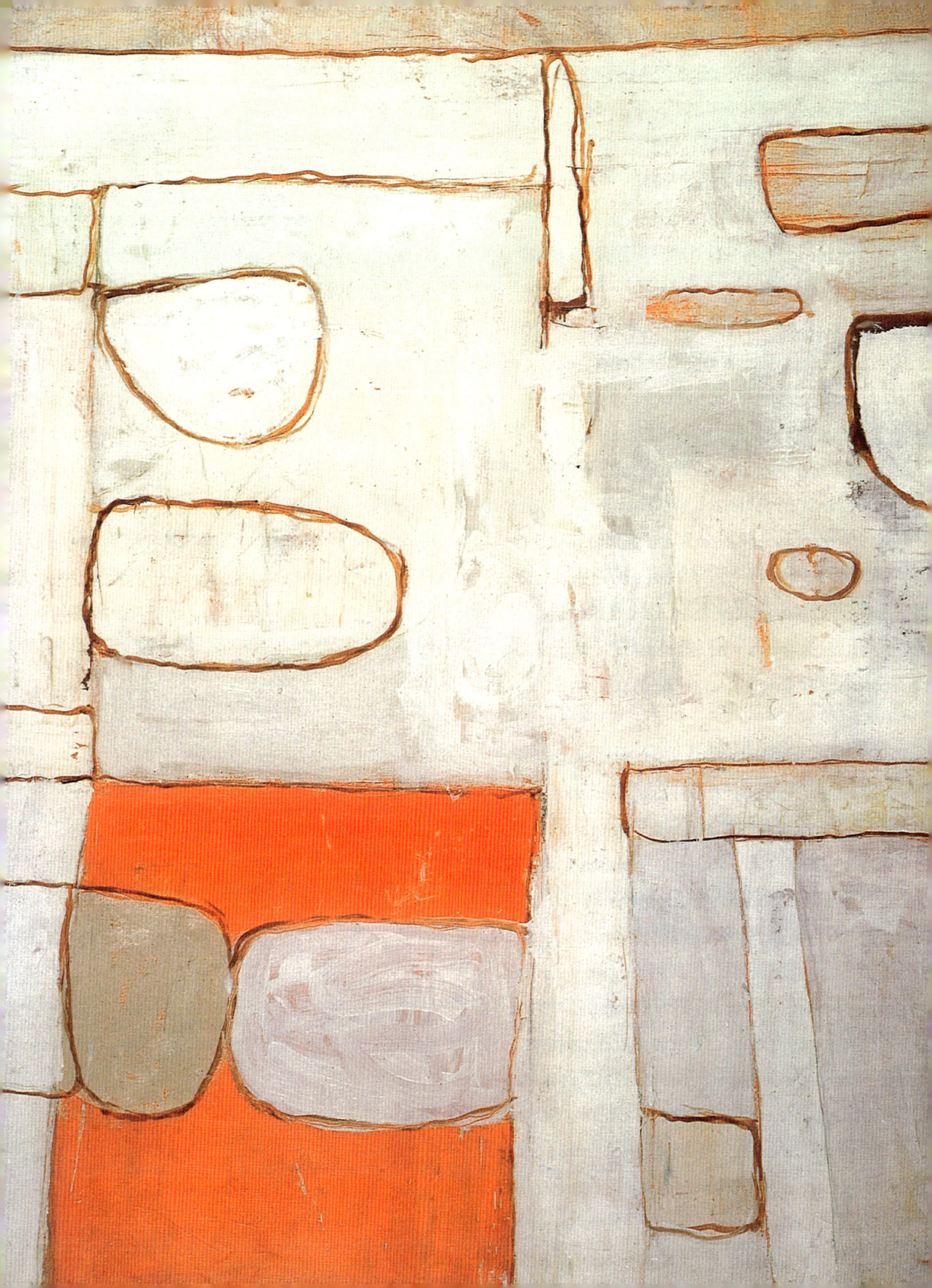

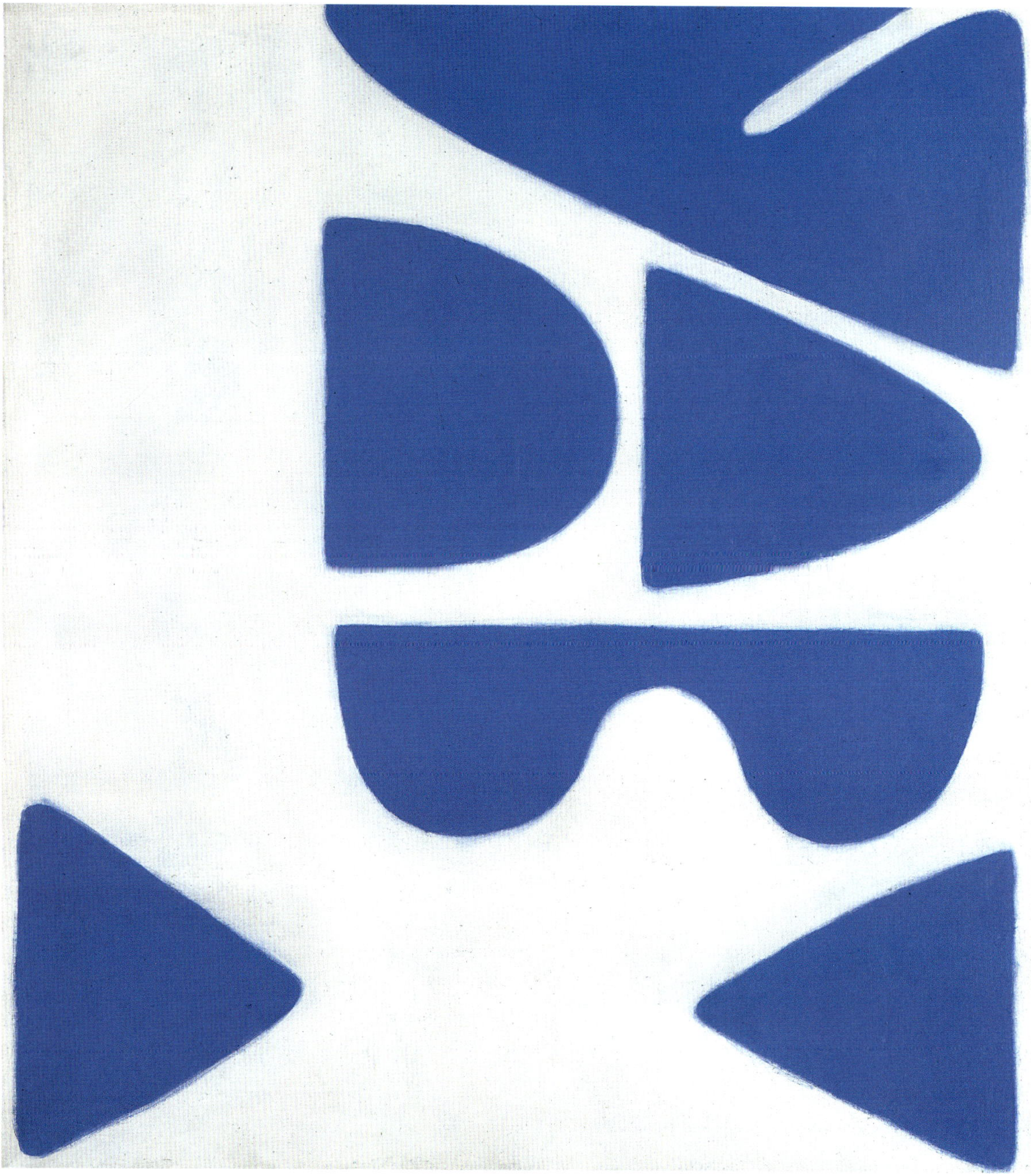

47

Berlin Blues 1, 1965, Oil on canvas, 160 x 173.3, Irish Museum of Modern Art, Dublin

5 LOOKING FORWARD, LOOKING BACK

ONE OF THE WAYS to measure the shifts in mood and taste during the late 1950s and early 1960s (one of the more volatile periods in British art) was to visit the John Moores Liverpool Exhibition, an event sponsored by the founder of the Littlewoods Company (based in Liverpool), which set out to display 'the best and most vital work being done today throughout the country'. It was also devised as a competition open to all. The first time it was held, in 1957, the social realists, represented by successful painters such as Jack Smith and John Bratby, walked off with the prizes. The second exhibition was held two years later in November 1959, and Scott won first prize in the British Painters section for *Blue Abstract* 1959. As his success proved, this time around the display looked very different, with abstract and near abstract paintings predominating. As one writer remarked, 'The simple and surprising reason is that Social Realism in England has almost disappeared... There has certainly been a sudden and very remarkable shift of emphasis in contemporary English art toward Abstract Expressionism in its many different forms – and for this the exhibitions of Pollock and the New York painters that we've seen have been in large measure responsible.'[44] Although this shift may seem unremarkable given Scott's experience of American art, the surprise registered by the writer at what was perceived as a sudden change is a reminder not only of the fickleness of taste, but also that even as late as 1959 British abstract artists were still regarded as a beleaguered minority.

It was true that recent exhibitions of Pollock and other New York painters had helped shift public opinion in favour of abstraction, but that was not the whole story. In July 1963, Scott received an invitation from Moritz von Bomhard, the Berlin representative of the Ford Foundation, to become an artist in residence in Berlin. The foundation was one of the institutions through which the CIA in America helped fund projects that, at the time of the Cold War, advanced the anti-communist cause. (The divisions of the Cold War were glaringly apparent in a Berlin divided by a wall into the democratic West and the communist East.) Abstract expressionism was the sort of painting that, as one writer has put it, 'spoke to a specifically anti-Communist ideology, the ideology of freedom, of free enterprise. Non-figurative and politically silent, it was the very antithesis to socialist realism.'[45] In the eyes of the Ford Foundation, Scott's position as a leading British abstract painter made him an obvious choice to help advance the aims of a long-running, covert cultural war. And covert it certainly was: Scott, just like André Masson, Emilio Vedova or Antonio Saura (three other abstract artists who participated in the artist-in residence programmes), would have had no idea about the involvement of the CIA, nor of the Ford Foundation's wider political agenda.

The Scotts arrived in West Berlin on 13 November 1963. They had been given a large furnished house within walking distance of the Ethnological Museum's collections in Dahlem, in the American sector of the city, cluttered with furniture and velvet curtains. As Scott told Martha Jackson in a letter written shortly after his arrival, 'We are very glad to be on this side of the wall and one can see why the Berliners are anxious it should stay so.' However, as time went on, Scott ventured out into East Berlin (he had no difficulty in crossing the checkpoints set up between the east and the west), and on his walks through the divided city he made several drawings of the wall. There were many distractions: the bars, which he loved (their decor reminded him of German expressionism), the political cabarets, concerts given by the Berlin Philharmonic and the Berliner Ensemble, and above all, the world-class collection of sculpture housed in the Egyptian Museum (now the Neues Museum). Scott was given a large studio in the Kunstakademie, and although he did not do a great deal of painting, he was able to work on a number of large-scale canvases (around nine oil paintings were delivered back to England, and when he cleared out his Berlin studio he is said to have destroyed about thirty or forty works on paper). The time spent away from England, in a city where the authorities

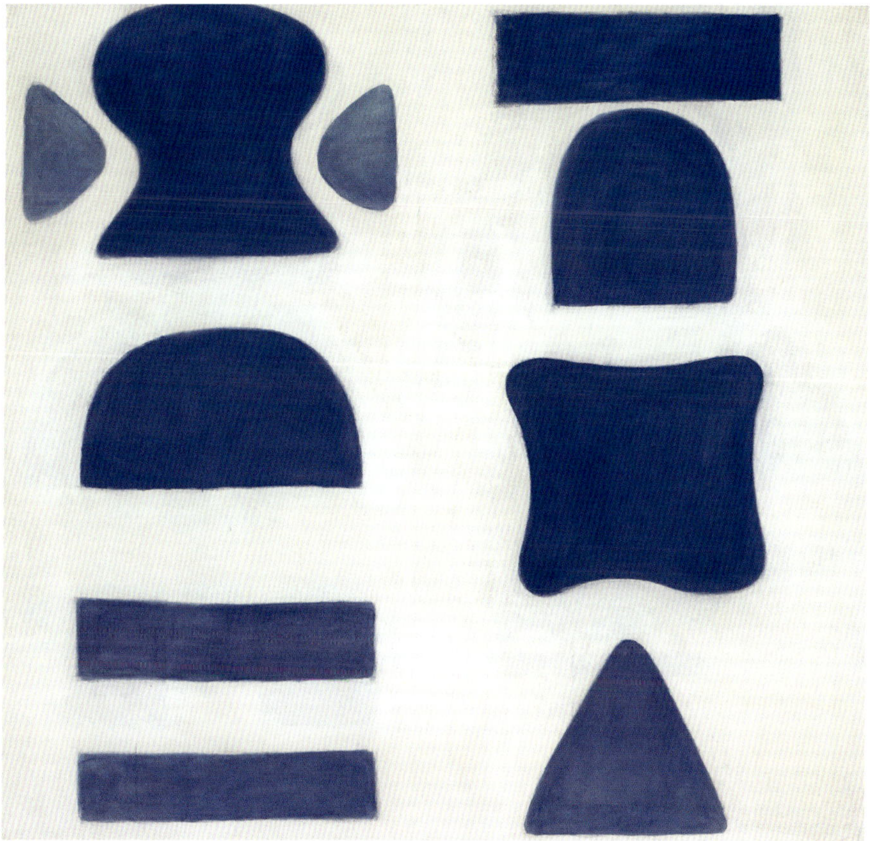

48
Berlin Blues 4
1965
Oil on canvas
153 x 183.5
Tate. Presented anonymously 1965

made sure that the recipients of a Ford grant were given every opportunity to enjoy what Berlin had to offer, had an exhilarating effect.

That exhilaration was expressed in a remarkable series of paintings called *Berlin Blues*, which he began in 1965 and completed the following year. These seven canvases, three of which are reproduced here (figs.47–9), are a reminder that even if Scott had more or less stopped making sculpture he had not stopped thinking like a sculptor. Unlike the forms in earlier works, which are either packed tightly together, solid and unmoving as in *Gaelic Landscape* (fig.50), for example, or loosely flowing as in *Nile Valley: Red and White*, those in *Berlin Blues 4* (fig.48) stand well apart from each other. They are abstract, vaguely geometric, but at the same time elusive, a combination that has something in common with Henry Moore's desire to carry 'a form as far as possible without having to define its significance'.[46] The most dynamic shape here is the triangle that sets up a thrusting

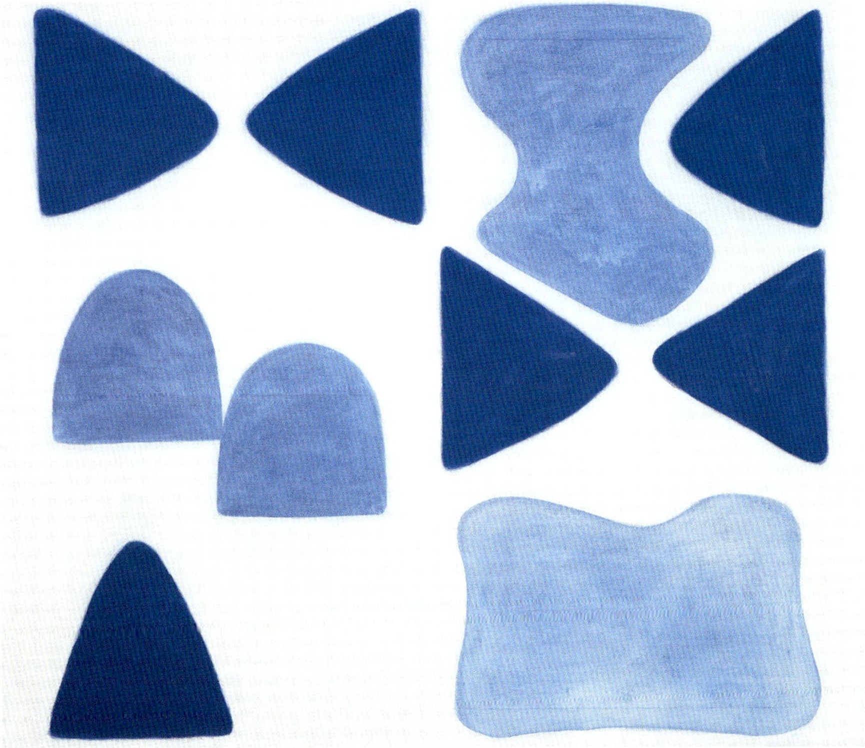

movement by entering from the side or confronting its pair head on. In the most ambitious of the series, *Berlin Blues 1*, there is a dramatic shift of weight to the right of the composition which Scott redresses by placing two triangular blocks, like ballast, either side of the bottom edge (fig.47). Even before he left for Berlin he would have been aware of the wave of new sculpture being made in Britain under the influence of Anthony Caro. Norbert Lynton has drawn attention to the similarities between the formal inventiveness of William Tucker's aluminium sculpture of around 1963 and the shapes in the *Berlin Blues*.[47] The analogy is fair, although Tucker, like Caro, was working with industrial materials that were riveted and welded together. Scott's forms, on the other hand, are much closer to Moore's in that they look as though they have been shaped by hand, either squeezed into a softly waisted pillow shape, as in the right hand side of *Berlin Blues 6* (fig.49), or coaxed into triangles and domes, the ends of which are rounded and blunt: no edge has the clean precision of aluminium or steel. On the contrary, the outlines are all slightly blurred with a penumbra of a paler blue, outlines made by applying layers of the blue paint, leaving the initial coat untouched around the edges. Whether the forms are distributed

49
Berlin Blues 6
1966
Oil on canvas
182.9 x 167.6
Arts Council Collection, Southbank Centre, London

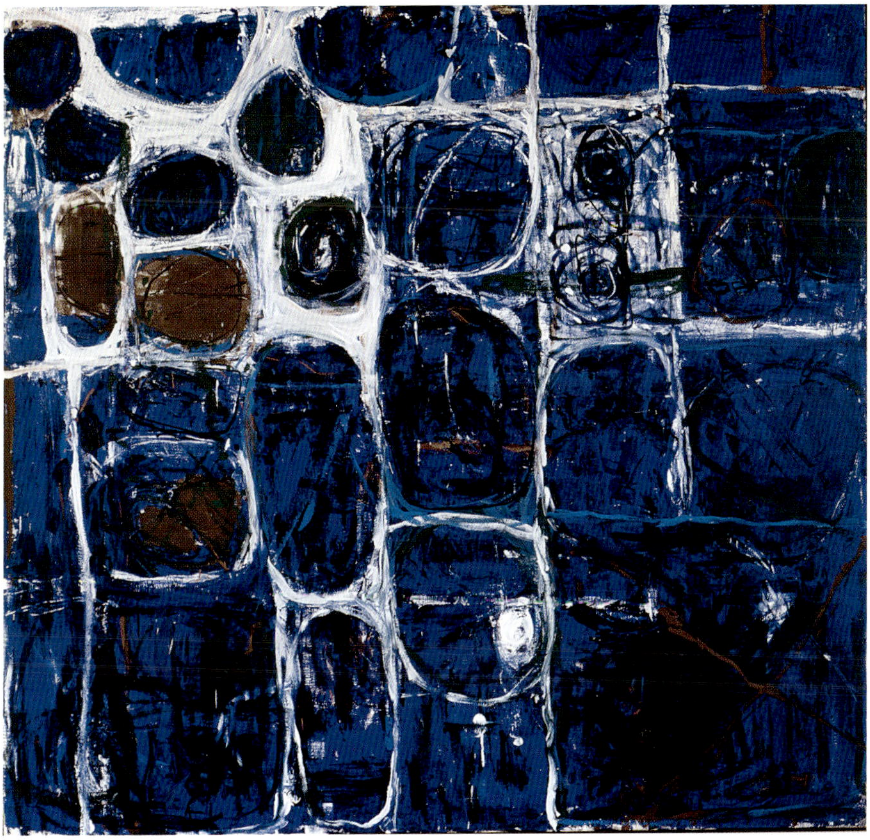

50
Gaelic Landscape
1961
Oil on canvas
160 x 174
Private collection

in an apparently random way or stacked vertically, they are far from inert. A sense of pressure is built up in the way each element balances its weight against another without a single form touching. It could well be the case that these radically different compositions were again arrived at by using cut-out pieces of paper, although, unlike with the method employed to compose the abstract paintings of the early 1950s and the Altnagelvin mural, this remains speculation. However, in 1972 Scott made a point of relating the *Berlin Blues* directly to his earlier mural saying that it was with a feeling of relief that now he could 'expand and go beyond the ties of easel painting'. In a sense, then, the series can be seen as the *equivalent* of a mural, not only in the way the canvases relate to one another but in the way they were shown, first in his exhibition at the Hanover Gallery in 1965 and again at the Tate Gallery retrospective in 1972. (It is greatly to be regretted that these paintings are now split up.) An installation shot of the room at the Tate show (fig.51) gives some idea of how the canvases work together, the syncopated rhythm of the forms bouncing between the

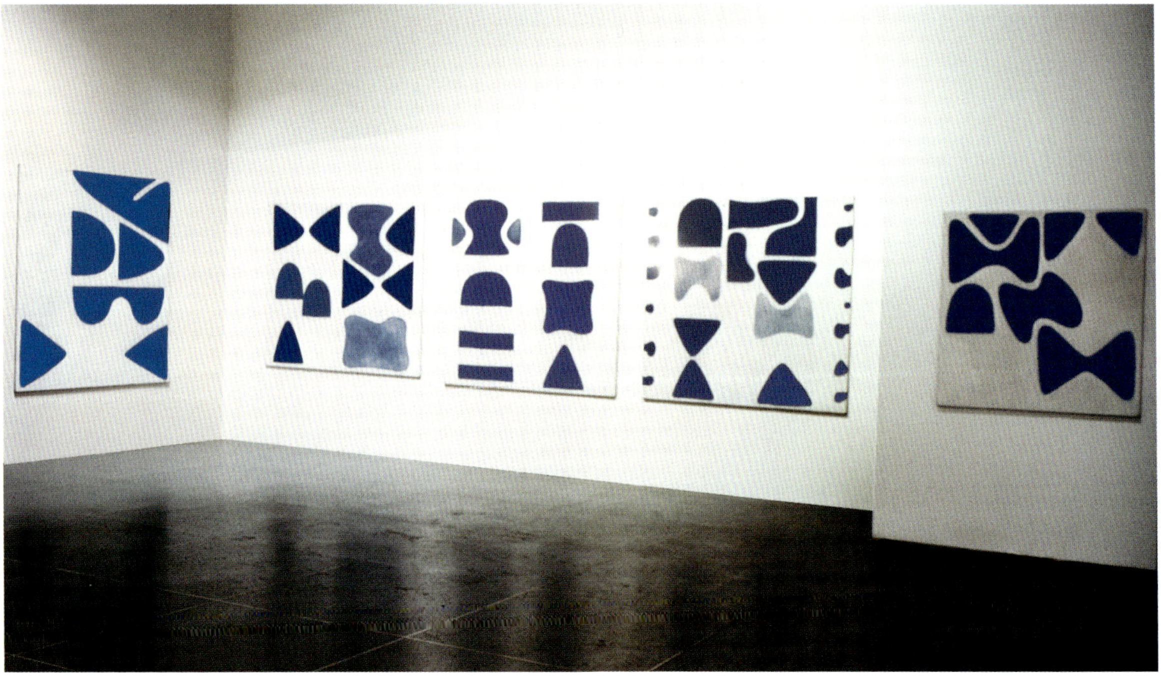

51
Installation view of William Scott's 1972 Tate Gallery exhibition

five paintings with the two vertical stacks in the middle acting as a sort of momentary pause for breath. That jazzlike improvisation accounts for the title, *Berlin Blues*, although when asked about the name Scott denied it had any significance 'apart from the discovery of this particular blue pigment in Berlin'.[48] But that cannot be the whole story. The melancholy note implicit in the title is obviously a reference to the plight of a city caught between two conflicting powers. Obvious too, is the link between the wall that separated East Berlin from the West and the idea of painting a 'wall', that is to say painting a group of canvases that when hung together could be seen as a mural. The 'particular blue pigment' Scott discovered in Berlin can be identified from a small tube found among the paints left in his studio: 'Pariserblau', one of the Mussini range of artists' colours produced by Schminke, a firm in Düsseldorf: it is the blue that dominates the series.

The emphatic frontality of the *Berlin Blues* marks a radical change from the drifting sensation that characterises paintings such as *Nile Valley: Red and White*. Movement is now intimated directly, through weight and balance. The two vertical stacks in *Green and Blue Forms* 1966 (fig.52), for example, appear to be static, but movement is suggested in their opposition to each other. In each, the weight is distributed differently,

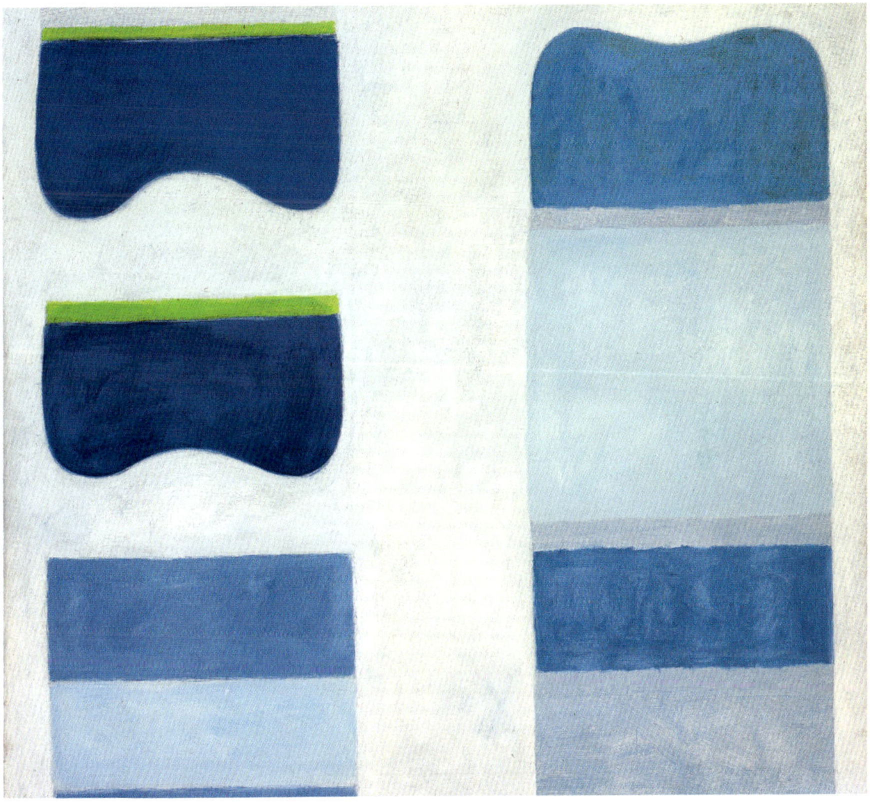

52
Green and Blue Forms
1966
Oil on canvas
168 x 183.5
Private collection

a downward thrust on the left (the forms springing apart), an upward thrust on the right where the forms are compressed together like the slabs of a column. Resolutely flat though the surface is, the three softly indented shapes give the illusion of roundness. In purely abstract terms, Scott's forms have something in common with contemporary sculpture, but it is also true that during this extremely fruitful period British sculpture itself was edging towards the painterly. The dancing rhythms of *Berlin Blues* have something of the boldness found in the extravagant flourishes of Philip King's metal sculptures of the early 1960s.

As Scott himself said, every one of his paintings was related to the one before: 'It may be a continuation of a previous painting or it may be a reaction against it.'[49] The improvisatory abstracts he was painting in the mid-1960s led to a return to still life, but to still life informed and distilled by the experience of space as well as pure form. In two large paintings, *Still Life Variations 2* 1969 (fig.53) and *Multi Blues* 1971 (fig.54) the large frying pan and the pots or round-bottomed bowls are suspended against a

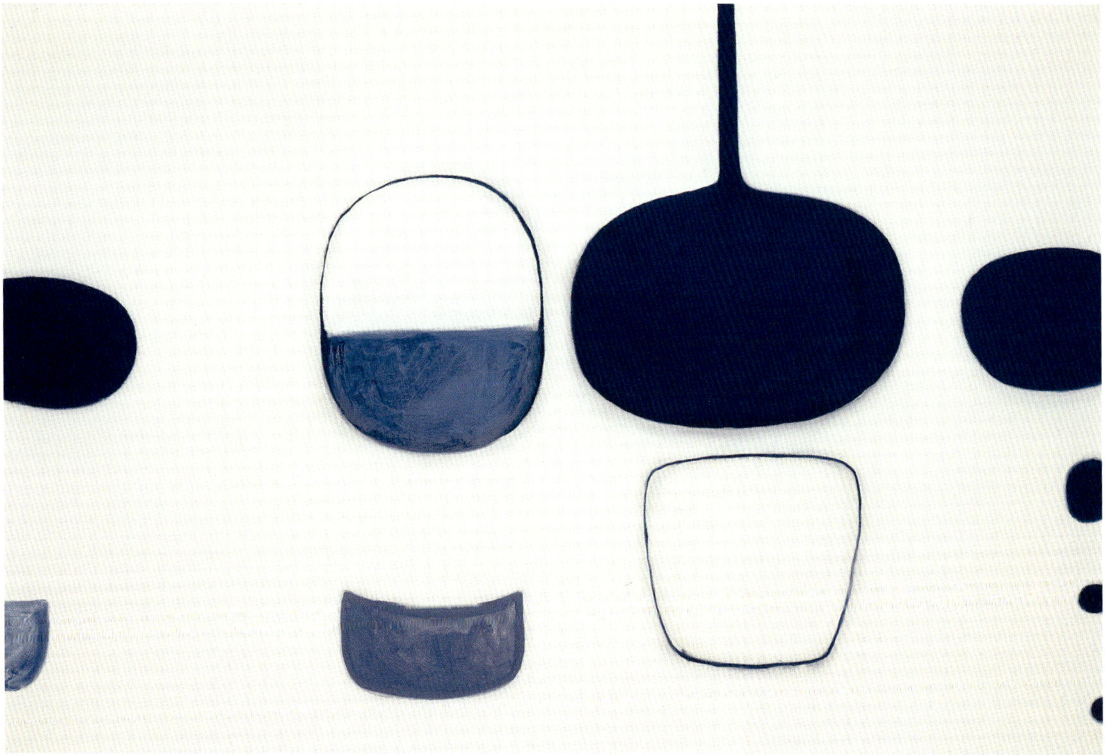

53
Still Life Variations 2
1969
Oil on canvas
121.9 x 182.9
Private collection

flat ground, held in place, as it were, by the rounded shapes, half obscured, lined up against the two vertical edges. It is always noticeable in Scott's still lifes how the structural tension of each composition is determined by the way the objects relate to the sides of the canvas. Scott himself used the phrase 'clinging to the edges' to describe the way small repeated forms inch their way in from the sides, like little intrusive presences. This structural device allowed him to open up the space at the centre of the composition, the space where the energy of the painting is most concentrated. In *Multi Blues*, for instance, it is the density of the space massed below the solid blocks of blue that allows the objects to hang in space as though suspended in mid-air.

In 1972 Scott was given a major retrospective at the Tate Gallery. It was organised by the gallery's director Alan Bowness, who allowed the artist to have a say in how it was to be arranged. The selection focused on twelve groups of works from crucial periods in the artist's career (nine groups of paintings, one of gouaches and two of drawings). As is often the case with living artists, it was the most recent works that invited the harshest criticism. Several of the critics, unanimous in their praise of the sumptuously painted

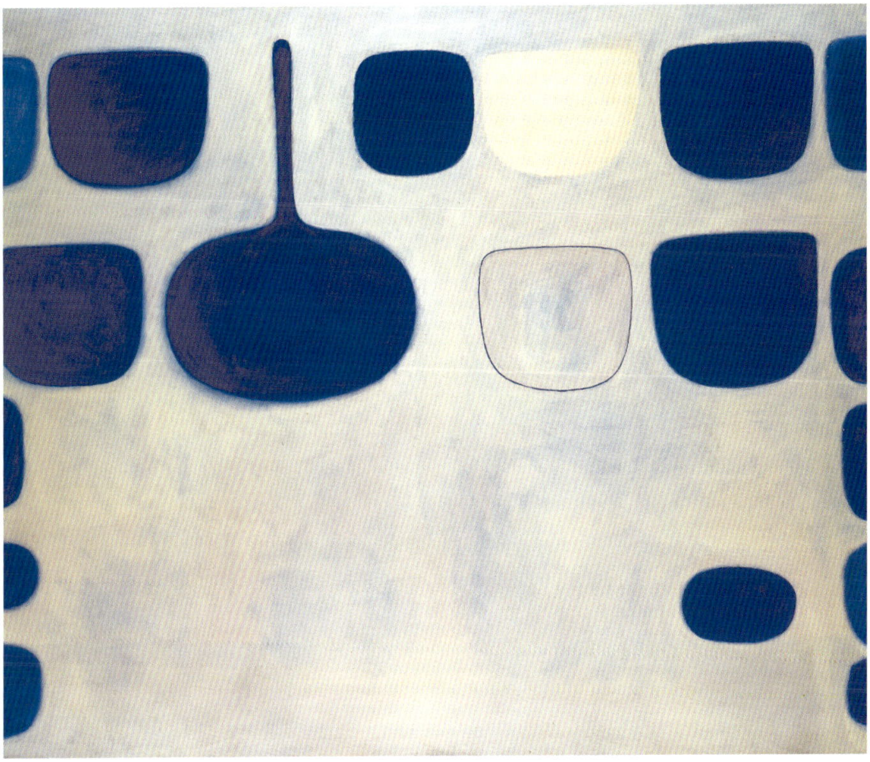

54
Multi Blues
1971
Oil on canvas
142.2 x 171.4
Private collection

still lifes of the late 1950s, were unable to understand the new works, finding the paint thin and diluted and the compositions oversimplified for their scale. Their grave beauty is best appreciated by standing in front of them, because, like a work by Rothko or Barnett Newman, the size of the canvas draws the spectator into the space. Scott's experience of painting the large mural for Altnagelvin had led him to believe that the audience should become physically part of a painting, that they should, as he put it, 'become integrated in its rhythm'. But the public can be unforgiving when an artist is seen to go against what are perceived to be his own instincts, and these large still lifes with their simple shapes laid out on a flat ground seemed to be aiming for the very perfection Scott had been so adamantly against a decade earlier. The signs of struggle and tension he had once actively sought to express through the act of painting had been replaced by a sense of balance and calm resolution.

He once said that when he went into the studio he did not think about whether he was going to paint a figure or a still life but whether he was going to fill a space or empty it out. Most striking about these late paintings is that he does both, emptying the canvas of all the detail of process yet

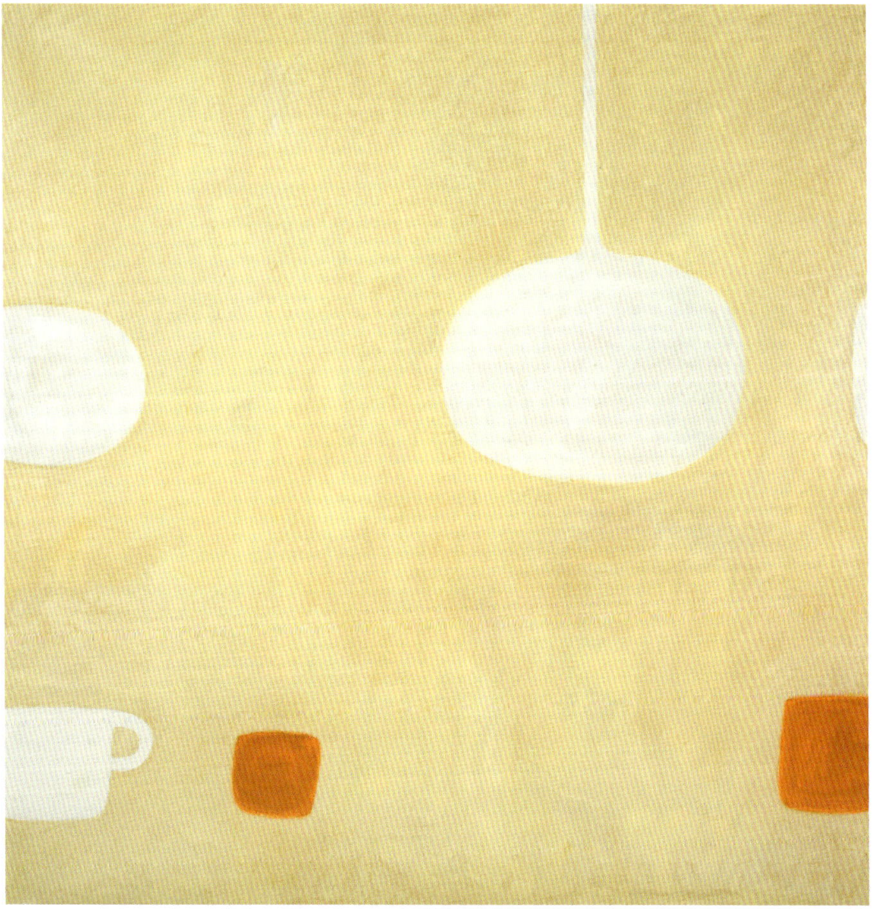

55
Orange Diminished
1973
Oil on canvas
122 x 122
Private collection

allowing the fullness of empty space to take its place. Whereas in a painting such as *Large Still Life* 1957, every pot and bowl seems caught at a moment of imminent transition, in *Orange Diminished* 1973 (fig.55) or *Egypt Series (No. 2)* 1972 (fig.56) the forms are fixed as though for eternity. The origins of this change can be traced as far back as 1956, when Scott visited Pompeii, outside Naples. It was, so he claimed, a moment of revelation. Encountering these ancient works for the first time, he said, made him realise that 'the Romans, working within the classical tradition could still achieve a great deal of what the primitives had achieved. They could make sculptures and paintings with the same directness that the primitives felt and remain classical.'[50] This visit came a year after Scott's momentous experience at Lascaux. What the two ancient sites had in common was large decorated walls: the rough-hewn painted surfaces of the Lascaux caves on the one hand, and the smooth frescoed walls of the houses at Pompeii on the other.

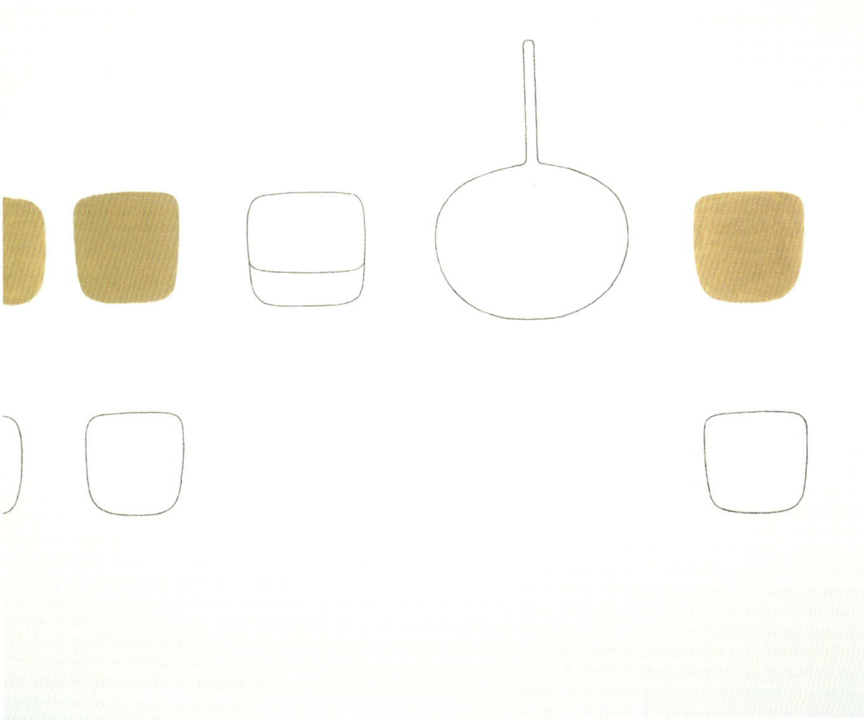

56
Egypt Series (No. 2)
1972
Oil on canvas
204 x 254
Albright-Knox Art Gallery, Buffalo, New York. Gift of Mr and Mrs David K Anderson, 1984

It was to be many years before he was able to bring together the mysterious language of signs found at Lascaux with the classical purity of Roman wall paintings, but these are the two experiences that surely lie behind Scott's large late still lifes, with their long wall-like formats and the carefully incised shapes on a uniformly painted background. 'The forms I use are the forms I see about me and the forms I have dreamt about since I was a child', he told an interviewer in 1954.[51] The frying pan, the object he regarded as his equivalent of Braque's guitar, hangs in many of these late works as a symbol of his childhood and of the life he claimed to know best.

At the same time as Scott was painting *Multi Blues* and *Egypt Series (No. 2)*, he was once again drawing from the model. Drawing was an exercise the purpose of which was to 'shock' himself out of too easy a rhythm, as he put it. 'I begin with no conception whatever. An image emerges, almost always an image I am obsessed with. I rub it out and begin again, searching for its counterpart. When it appears, I invariably find the thing I draw is at my elbow; it is out of the window, or has been standing at my feet for a long time.'[52] A small still life drawing (fig.57) gives some idea of that obsession, the rubbing out, the beginning again, more rubbing out followed invariably

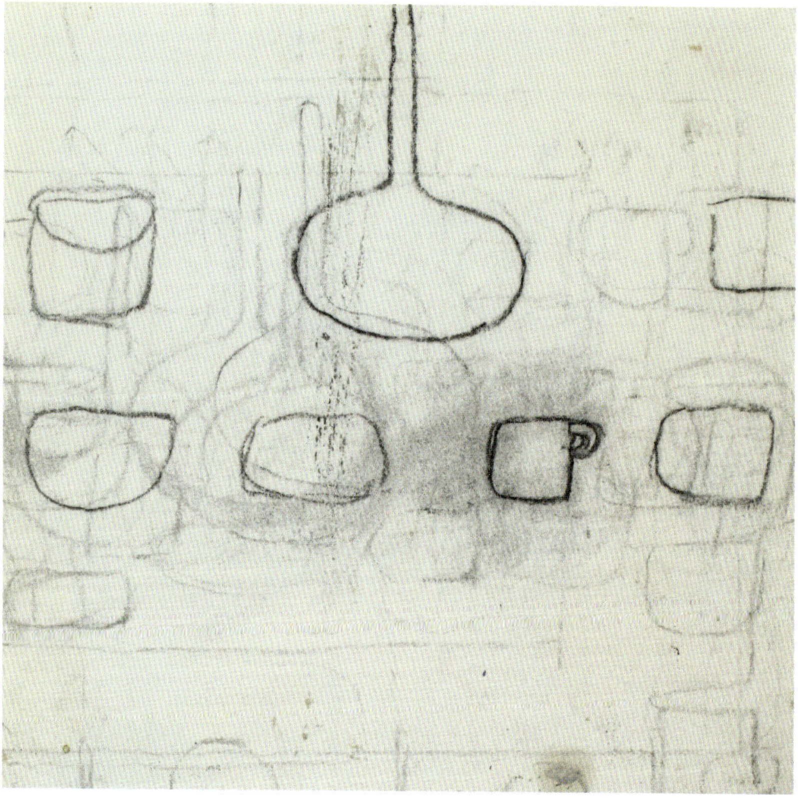

57
Study
1970
Charcoal on paper
27.9 x 29.2
Private collection

by a return to the point of departure. A close inspection of some of the late still-life paintings reveals that lying beneath what appears to be a pristine surface are faint charcoal lines charting the artist's changes of mind as he shifts a form this way and that, leaving traces of discarded efforts that are incorporated into the final image. It is as though leaving out the history of all the decisions that go into making a composition somehow diminished the integrity of the finished work. (The 'integrity' of a work of art was an idea widely held at the time, particularly among the abstract expressionists: Clyfford Still, for example, maintained that the artist had to accept total responsibility for everything he executed.)[53] *Nine Illustrations of Form* 1971 (fig.58) is a very different type of drawing. In fact, *Nine Illustrations* cannot really be called a drawing: it is a large work on canvas with the ground painted in oils. Using a stick of charcoal, Scott draws lines that are delicate, precise and fluid. The composition is a grid made up of nine squares each filled with part of a female nude. The sections of the body have the fragmentary quality of damaged antiquities in which outlines are flawlessly incised into a piece of plaster or limestone, like those found on

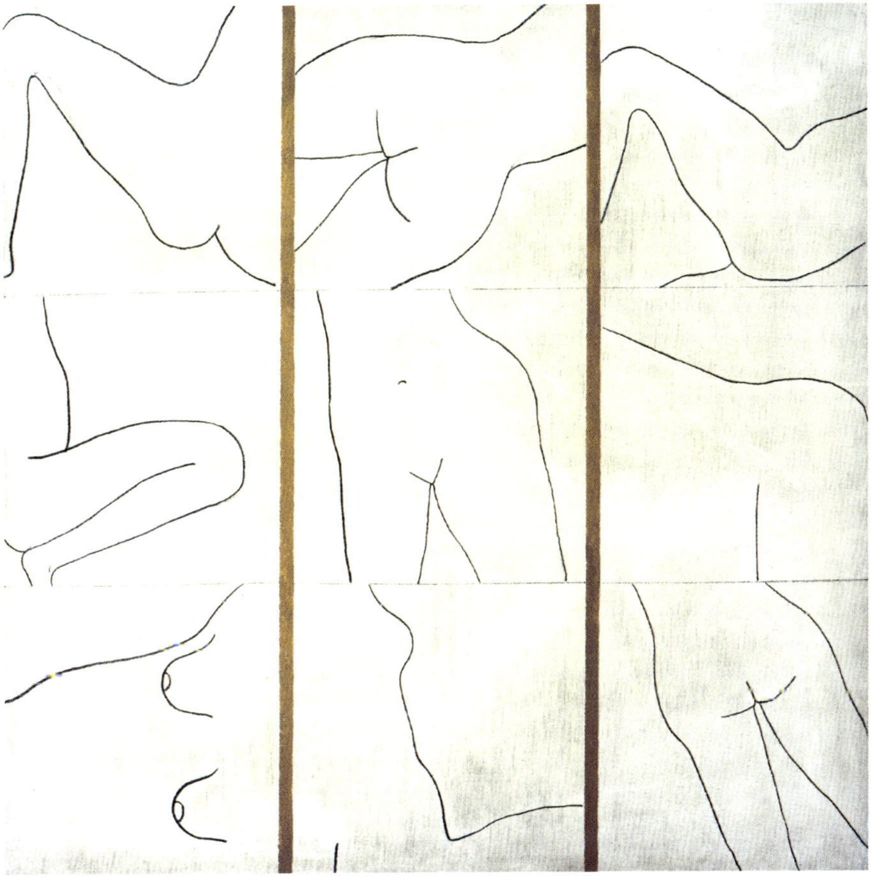

58
Nine Illustrations of Form
1971
Oil and charcoal on canvas
169.3 x 173.1
Private collection

the Egyptian low-relief carvings that Scott believed to be 'some of the most beautiful drawings ever made'. The nude (the fragments seem to belong to the same body) stands, reclines, squats, kneels and lies back with one leg raised, each position recorded in the gentlest of curved lines. In the middle section of the panel on the right, the body is pared down to a mere two lines, the barest possible description but enough to leave the whisper of a lower back at the point where the hip joins the buttock. Scott loved the female body. He took many photographs of his models, drew them constantly and, when there was no model to hand, turned to his collection of nude magazines. The variety of positions in *Nine Illustrations* brings out the close bond that builds up between an artist and his model (in this instance the model was a young American student): the way Scott moves around the model and the way she changes position, now on her front, now on her side, allows the viewer to share an intimacy that is both private and public. The individual drawings, although realised on a large scale, have

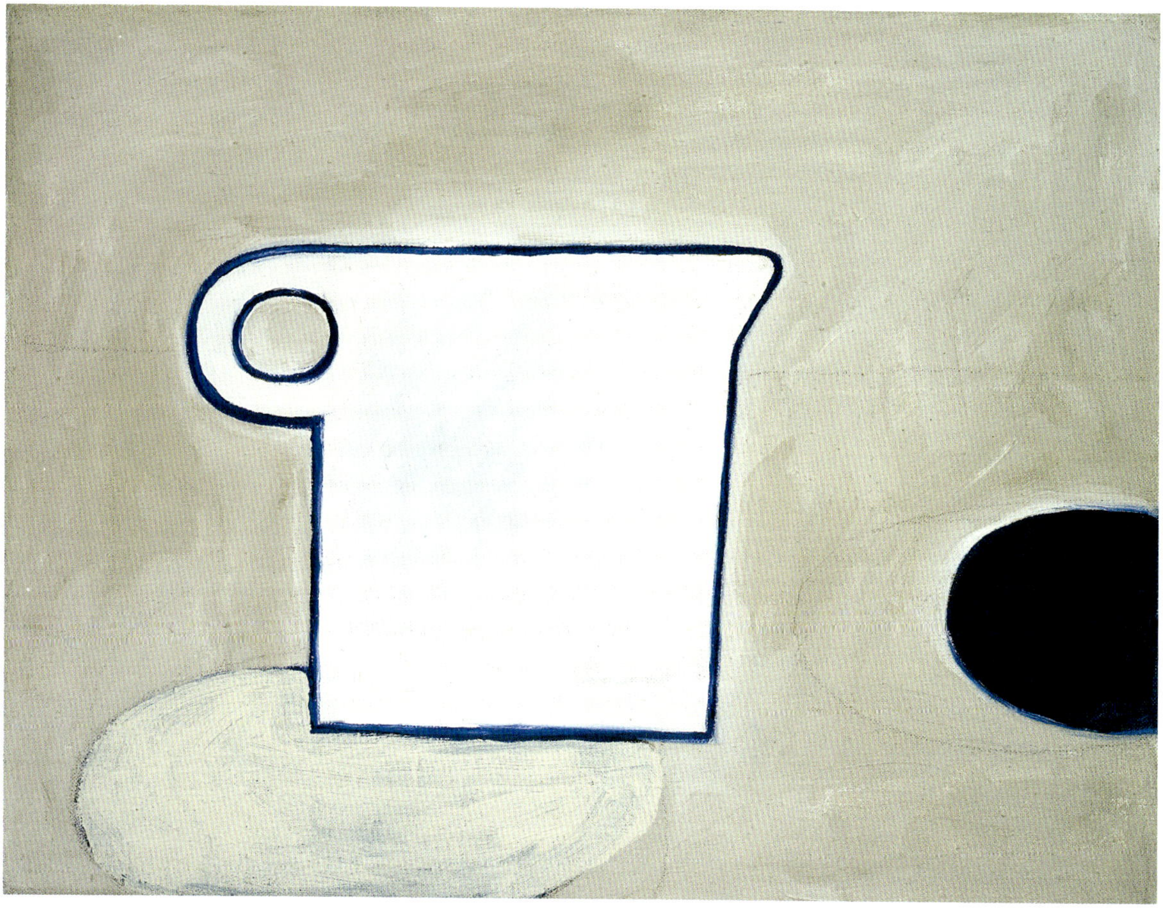

59
Poem for a Jug
1979
Oil on canvas
30.6 x 40.9
Private collection

the feel of pages taken from a sketchbook. As it happens, a few months before Scott painted *Nine Illustrations*, he was working on a small book made up of eleven line drawings painted in cobalt blue and accompanied by five erotic poems by the writer and critic Edward Lucie-Smith. The book, *A Girl Surveyed*, was published by the Hanover Gallery in March 1971. Scott had thought of using poems he had written himself but had been dissuaded from doing so by his gallery. (He had also begun writing a script for a play in twelve short acts to be performed over ten minutes by three voices on an unlit stage. If this sounds like an idea inspired by Samuel Beckett it is worth remembering that Beckett had been a pupil at Portora Royal School in Scott's hometown of Enniskillen.)

The mixture of finely executed line drawings and erotic subject matter may well have grown out of Scott's growing interest in Japanese art,

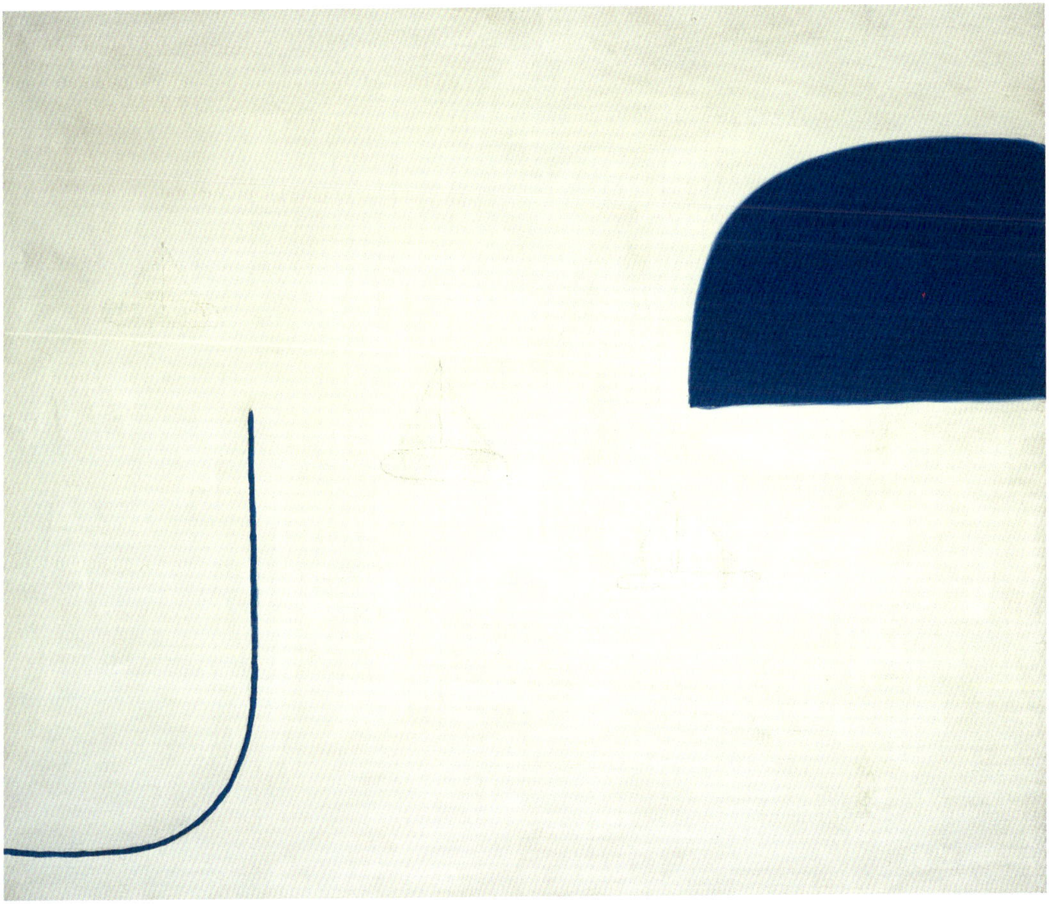

60
Harbour
1976
Oil on canvas
63.5 x 76.2
Private collection

including modern Japanese erotic literature collected on a trip to Japan in 1976. Alongside the large oils of the late years are two groups of much smaller works, both conceived as series. *An Orchard of Pears* and *Poem for a Jug* (fig.59) feature, as the titles suggest, still-life subjects, but they are not exactly still lifes. They are more like pictorial archetypes, a single jug standing in for the kitchen still life, a solitary pear for a bowl of fruit. These extreme distillations of the still-life theme, which had begun with large-scale works such as *Linear Still Life* 1973, bring Scott's career to its close. As the scale of the works became reduced to a single motif, so did Scott's mind gradually begin to lose its lucidity. The last five years or so of his life were blighted by Alzheimer's and by 1986 he had stopped painting altogether. Nevertheless, according to his son James, even when he could no longer recognise his immediate family, he could remember paintings, and on seeing an image could immediately identify the artist.

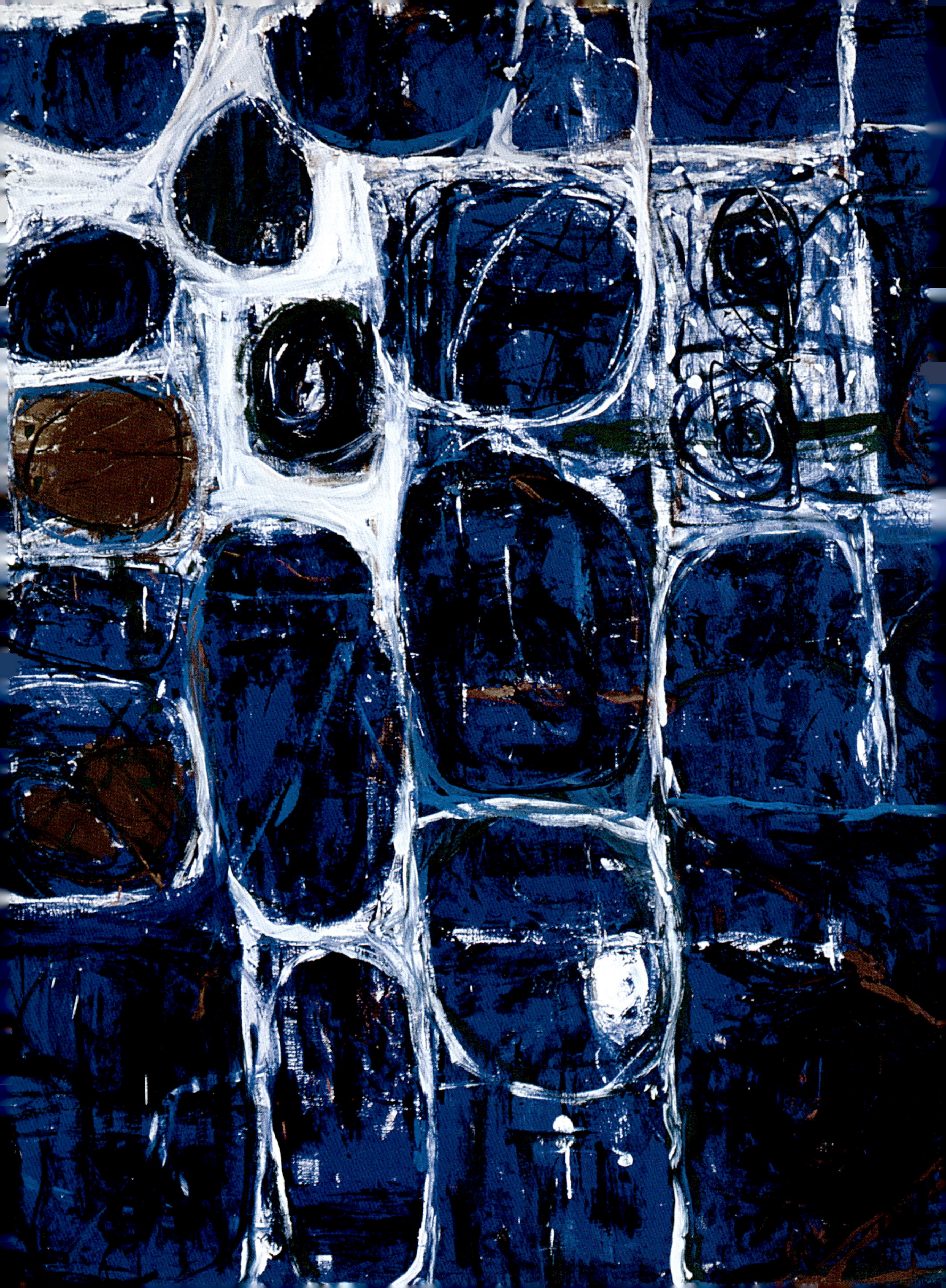

6 AFTERWORD

Gaelic Landscape
1961 (detail of fig.50)

ONE OF THE CONSEQUENCES of a long and successful career is that an artist may live to see his reputation falter. This is what happened to Scott, and to others of his generation. In 1977, at the time of a large survey exhibition, *British Art 1952–1977* at the Royal Academy of Arts in London, Scott's great friend Patrick Heron wrote to a member of the Arts Council complaining, 'What we are up against is the largely unconscious criterion which seems to preclude my entire generation from all serious surveys of British painting after 1960.'[54] Around the same time, Scott told one of the curators at the Tate Gallery that he regretted that painters of his generation had lacked 'an apt name', a recognisable tag such as 'St Ives School' (a group, as it happens, he strenuously denied being a part of). The implication of that remark is that being identified with a group made it easier for artists to attract the attention of critics and art historians (an idea amply justified by the history of the past hundred years or so). As they get older, most artists who attain the levels of recognition that both Scott and Heron enjoyed at the height of their fame will always be sensitive to changes in their critical standing. Nevertheless, their anxiety was justified. Scott was barely mentioned in Frederick Gore's wide-ranging essay in the catalogue of the 1977 exhibition of British art mentioned above, even though he was for many years one of the most prominent artists working in Britain and recognised as such both in America and Europe. Nor does his name appear in the *Dictionary of British Art* published in 1985 (which included his contemporaries such as Heron, Roger Hilton, Peter Lanyon and Anthony Hill). Perhaps the biggest blow came when Scott was left out altogether from *British Art in the 20th Century: The Modern Movement* , a major survey organised by Norman Rosenthal in 1987, which, once again, took place at the Royal Academy. It is not difficult to see the reasons behind this gradual diminution of interest. Scott was born into a generation of artists that would find themselves overwhelmed not only by the explosion of different art forms beginning with pop art in the late 1950s and early 1960s, but also by the myriad questioning that followed about what art was and the multiplicity of what it could now be. As one writer put it, the neglect that Scott and others suffered came from being unfashionably steeped in the European tradition.[55]

Nor can it have helped that as time went by Scott's work began to be seen in the context of modern design. At the height of his fame, several of Scott's collectors were prominent architects, such as Basil Spence and Eugene Rosenberg in Britain and Ronald Tallon in Dublin, with the result that from the 1950s on his work became closely associated with a certain type of modernist architecture and interior design. (In the 1960s several photographers, including Norman Parkinson, borrowed his paintings for advertising shoots to give their interiors an authentic 'modern' feel). This may have seemed desirable at the time – and led to more than one important commission – but it became less so when, with hindsight, the era of the Festival of Britain began to look bleak and dreary, and worse, conservative and middle-aged when compared with the super-charged energy of the youthful decades that followed.

The upshot is that if ever an artist's reputation was in urgent need of rescuing it is Scott's. He is often said to have been a painter whose aim was to steer a course between figuration and abstraction, and this was taken by some critics to betray a doubt in the artist's mind as to whether abstract shapes on the canvas could have their own validity. To suggest a lack of conviction on Scott's part is wholly to misunderstand his intentions. It would be far truer to say that in pursuing both the abstract and the figurative he was looking for a way of immersing his art in the elemental and primitive without losing sight of the fact that he belonged to the figurative tradition he had always revered. Steeped in European art he certainly was, but this never prevented him from borrowing whatever he needed from other times and other cultures. In this respect, he has more in common with English sculptors such as Moore and William Turnbull, for example, than he does with his fellow painters. Looking back on his career, one can observe that from early on Scott began to see the world through symbols and signs rather than through objects for their own sake. He spoke about 'the secret in the picture', a quality of mystery or emotion that lends a still life, say, or a figure study, something that cannot be immediately grasped or understood. It was his way of keeping the commonplace at bay. His understanding that the primitive and the classical need not be opposed to each other had been the insight he took away from the Roman frescos at Pompeii. The belief that nothing really separates the art of the past, however remote, from the art of the present explains the way his repertoire of shapes evolved over the years from the familiar and recognisable objects of the early still lifes to the clustering jugs and pots of the mid-1950s, to the elemental shapes of the later paintings, and finally to his fixation on the single, emblematic object. He once said that when he tried to make a purely abstract picture, 'dividing the canvas into the right shapes and proportions', he nearly always failed (the *Berlin Blues* series is one great exception).[56] However abstract his images, they are nearly always extrapolated from objects and places that had been with him since his earliest years. A painting such as *Harbour* 1976 (fig.60), for instance, consists of two forms that are so elemental their meaning or purpose seem impossible to grasp. Nonetheless, the title allows the curved forms to be interpreted as signs of shelter and protection. And once this is understood, it becomes apparent how frequently the curved form occurs in Scott's painting, whether it is the frying pan, the bowl, the plate or the pear. Each of these objects represents life at its most simple. Given Scott's austere beginnings, it would not be surprising if pursuing a life in art had been his way of sheltering and protecting himself from an unwelcome reality, and that the objects he chose to paint were those that reminded him, however unconsciously, of a world that was familiar and secure. 'Of course,' he once explained, 'what I hope is that one day all my things will become so involved, so tangled together, that I will just go on painting without thinking either figure, still life or landscape and hope that they will contain all the experience of the past.'[57]

NOTES

1 *Murray's Handbook for Travellers in Ireland*, London 1912, p.165.
2 In 1972, when the BBC was making a film about Scott for the *Review* programme (to coincide with the Tate Gallery retrospective exhibition), Scott noted down his memories of his early life in Enniskillen. William Scott Archive.
3 Ibid.
4 'Kathleen Bridle Talks to T.P. Flanagan', transcript of filmed interview, c.1980.
5 Letter from Scott Medd to his mother, 23 June 1933. Trent University Archives, Medd 81-001/3/3.
6 Mervyn Levy, 'The Artist at Work: 8. William Scott's Circle and Square', *Studio*, vol.164, no.832, Aug. 1962.
7 His criticism of Klee is interesting because around this date Scott is said to have shared an exhibition with the Swiss painter at the Foyer Gallery in the Hampstead Everyman Cinema. No confirmation of the exhibition has been found.
8 Elsbeth Juda, in conversation, 2008.
9 Roland Gant, 'Spear and Banner', *Tribune*, 22 Feb. 1946.
10 Letter from Scott to 'George', 24 Feb. 1952. William Scott Archive.
11 Elsbeth Juda, in conversation, 2008.
12 British Council Recorded Lecture, 1959. A copy of the script is in the William Scott Archive.
13 Ibid.
14 *L'Atelier de Corot (Jeune femme au corsage rouge)*, c.1865–6. Musée d'Orsay, Paris. The Corot painting was acquired by the Musées Nationaux in 1933, and Scott would have been able to see it in the Louvre on visits to Paris before and after the war. It was also included in the long-running exhibition *Chefs d'oeuvre de la Peinture Française au Louvre* that opened in June 1946 (closed March 1952).
15 Philip James, 'Patronage for Paintings '51', *Studio*, Aug. 1951, p.47.
16 British Council Recorded Lecture, 1959.
17 Scott later showed twenty of these gouaches at the Hanover Gallery in May–June 1962.
18 Paul Feiler, in conversation with the author, 2008.
19 Information kindly given to the author by Howard Hodgkin.
20 The photographs were almost certainly taken by Martha Jackson, or with her camera, as they are part of the Martha Jackson Archive, Buffalo, New York.
21 British Council Recorded Lecture, 1972. A copy of the script is in the William Scott Archive.
22 Ibid.
23 Letter from Martha Jackson to Scott, 25 Sept. 1953. William Scott Archive.
24 Letter from Martha Jackson to Scott, 18 Feb. 1957. William Scott Archive. This new market for English and European painting did not always work to Scott's advantage. Giving him the sobering news that his paintings had not sold very well, Martha Jackson explained that 'Peter Lanyon and Alan Davie's paintings being practically abstract and colourful are more acceptable to the American taste than your dark paintings, figures or nudes.'
25 Jo Gee (Diamond) in conversation with the author.
26 Statement published in *The New Decade*, exh. cat., Museum of Modern Art, New York, 1955. Reprinted in Theo Crosby, 'William Scott', *Architectural Design*, June 1957.
27 British Council Recorded Lecture, 1959.
28 Patrick Heron, 'Colour and Abstraction in the Drawings of Bonnard', *Bonnard. Drawings from 1893–1946*, American Federation of Arts, New York (touring exh.), 1972.

29 Pierre Bonnard's diary, 2 Dec. 1935. Reserve des Bibliothèque nationale, Paris.

30 'The Arts', *Times*, 12 Aug. 1955.

31 Martha Jackson described the installation in a letter to Scott, 28 Aug. 1954: 'The shipment came and everything looked stunning together. There is a curious something in common. The black Bacons, the white marble Hepworths, and the austere commanding black-and-white Scotts. It couldn't look more terrific. Each has a strong primitive insight. Hepworth's entirely feminine, and an authority and elegance only seen in British art.'

32 British Council Recorded Lecture, 1959.

33 Ibid.

34 Letter from Scott to Mary Chamot, 31 May 1961. Mary Chamot, Dennis Farr and Martin Butlin, *Modern British Paintings, Drawings and Sculpture*, vol. II, Tate Gallery, London, 1964, p.612.

35 *5,000 Years of Egyptian Art*, organised by the Arts Council of Great Britain, opened at the Royal Academy of Arts, on 22 June (closed 12 Aug.).

36 There is no record of Scott visiting Egypt.

37 John Russell (introduction), *William Scott*, exh. cat., Hanover Gallery, London, 1961, n.p.

38 Rothko came over for the opening, and he and the Scotts met for dinner on 2 October. The following week the two painters visited Henry Moore at Perry Green.

39 Peter Selz, 'Mark Rothko', in *Mark Rothko: A Retrospective Exhibition. Paintings 1945–1960*, exh. cat., Whitechapel Art Gallery, London, Oct.–Nov. 1961, p.20.

40 From a letter written jointly by Rothko and Adolph Gottlieb to the *New York Times*, 13 June 1943.

41 Pierre Rouve, 'William Scott', *Arts Review*, 3 June 1961, p.11.

42 The typescript of the scenario by Eric Jones is in the William Scott Archive.

43 *The New American Painting*, exh. cat., Tate Gallery, London, 1959, p.11.

44 Alan Bowness, 'London', *ARTS*, Jan. 1960, p.16.

45 Frances Stonor Saunders, *The Cultural Cold War: The CIA and the World of Arts and Letters*, New York, 2001.

46 Philip James (ed.), *Henry Moore on Sculpture*, London, 1966, p.205.

47 'William Scott', *Modern British Masters* series, London, 1990.

48 Letter from William Scott to the Tate Gallery, 25 Nov. 1965.

49 Lawrence Alloway, *Nine Abstract Artists: Their Work and Theory*, London, 1954.

50 British Council Recorded Lecture, 1959.

51 Alloway 1954.

52 British Council Recorded Lecture, 1959.

53 Lawrence Alloway, 'Notes on the Paintings', in *Some Paintings from the E.J. Power Collection*, exh. cat., Institute of Contemporary Arts, London, March–April 1958.

54 Letter from Patrick Heron to Joanna Drew, 21 June 1977.

55 Eddie Wolfram, review of *William Scott*, in *Art & Artists*, May 1972, p.49.

56 British Council Recorded Lecture, 1959

57 Ibid.

CHRONOLOGY

1913
Born in Greenock, Scotland, 15 February, the first boy of the three children born to William George Scott and his wife Agnes. Between 1913 and 1928 the couple had seven more children, the last one born after Scott's father died in an accident.

1924–8
The family moved to Enniskillen, County Fermanagh. Scott attended the local Model school, and within a few years was benefiting from classes given locally by Kathleen Bridle, a graduate of the Royal College of Art, London. Following the death of his father in 1927, Scott enrolled at the Belfast School of Art.

1931–9
Scott entered the Royal Academy Schools, London, as a sculpture student, transferring to the Painting School in 1934. After leaving the RA Schools in 1935, Scott married a fellow student, Mary Lucas, and the couple moved to France in 1937 where they set up a short-lived School of Painting in Pont-Aven, Brittany. They returned to England in August 1939, just before the outbreak of war.

1941–6
Scott took a part-time teaching post at Bath School of Art, before serving in the Royal Army Ordnance Corps for the duration of the war. He had his first solo exhibition at the Leger Galleries in September 1942, followed by a second exhibition there in February 1945. In 1946 Scott painted the first of his 'Frying pan' pictures, the start of his preoccupation with still life. In the autumn of that year, he was appointed Senior Painting Master at the Bath Academy of Art.

1948–58
Scott met the painter Patrick Heron, who became a lifelong friend. In the course of 1952 his work became more abstract. In August 1953 he visited New York where, thanks to the gallery owner, Martha Jackson, who was to represent him in America, he met a number of leading painters such as Jackson Pollock, Willem de Kooning and Mark Rothko. Around the mid 1950s Scott started experimenting with cut out pieces of paper as a means of composition, a method he was to use repeatedly from then on. Seeing the Paleolithic drawings in the caves at Lascaux, in 1954, and the Roman frescoes at Pompeii in 1956, were experiences that significantly affected Scott's later work. In 1958, he represented Great Britain at the Venice Biennale. Many of his most densely-worked 'table-top still lifes' date from the late 1950s.

1960–70
A commission for a large mural for Altnagelvin Hospital in Londonderry completed in 1961 heralded a series of ambitious abstract paintings, among them the *Berlin Blues* series, painted after a period spent in Berlin in 1963–4.

1972–89
In 1972 the Tate Gallery gave Scott his first major retrospective exhibition. By now Scott was an artist with a solid international reputation whose work could be seen in major museums both in America and Europe. The large emblematic still lifes of the 1970s gave way to series of smaller canvases treating a single theme such as *Orchard of Pears* and *Poem for a Jug*, subjects greatly influenced by his discovery of Japanese art. By 1985 Scott was showing signs of Alzheimer's. He died on 28 December 1989 at his home in Coleford, Somerset.

SELECT BIBLIOGRAPHY

MONOGRAPHS

Ronald Alley, *William Scott*, London 1963

Alan Bowness, *William Scott: Paintings*, London 1964

Norbert Lynton, *William Scott*, London 2004

STATEMENTS BY THE ARTIST

Lawrence Alloway, *Nine Abstract Artists: Their Work and Theory*, London 1954

Andrew Carnduff Ritchie (ed.), *The New Decade – 22 European Painters and Sculptors*, exh. cat., Museum of Modern Art, New York 1955

Script of British Council Recorded Lecture, 1959, William Scott Archive

Peter Lanyon, Alan Davie and William Scott talking to David Sylvester about their work, BBC

recording 19 June 1959 (Tate Archive TAV 214AB)
Mervyn Levy, 'William Scott's Circle and Square: The perennial theme', *The Studio*, August 1962
'Biographical Notes' in *William Scott*, exh. cat., Tate Gallery, London 1972
Script of talk on drawing given on the occasion of the Perth Prize for Drawing International, The Art Gallery of Western Australia, Perth, Australia, 1973, (unpublished). William Scott Archive
'The Artist Talks about his Painting', The British Council Recorded Sound Section, Tape 1885, 30 April 1974 (published in *William Scott*, exh. cat., Mcaffrey Fine Art, New York 2010)
'William Scott in conversation with Tony Rothon', *Studio International*, December 1974
'Introduction by William Scott', in Lou Klepac (ed.), *William Scott Drawings*, New York 1975
'Interview with William Scott', Imperial War Museum Sound Archive, 1981. Accession no. 4831
'William Scott in Conversation with Ciaran Ciarty', *Sunday Tribune*, Belfast, 24 August 1986

SELECTED ARTICLES

Patrick Heron, 'William Scott', *New Statesman and Nation*, 20 June 1953
Myfanwy Piper, 'Object Lessons', *Sunday Times*, 30 September 1956
Theo Crosby, 'William Scott', *Architectural Design*, June 1957
John Berger, 'Tooths and Bones', *New Statesman*, 22 September 1958
David Sylvester, [review of Hanover 1961], *New Statesman*, 2 June 1961
John Russell, 'William Scott', *London Magazine*, vol.1, no.3, June 1961
Pierre Rouve, 'William Scott', *Arts Review*, June 1961
Robert Melville, 'William Scott', *Motif 8*, Winter 1961
Mervyn Levy, 'William Scott's Circle and Square: A Perennial Theme', *Studio*, vol.1964, no.832, August 1962
Keith Sutton, 'William Scott', *Cimaise*, January 1963
David Sylvester, 'British Painting Now', *Sunday Times Colour Magazine*, 2 June 1963
Max Kozloff, 'British Painting Today', *Encounter*, January 1964
John Russell, 'Objects of magic', *Sunday Times*, 23 April 1972
Brian Ferran, 'Man from the North', *Irish Times*, 3 May 1972
Peter Campbell, 'Still-Lifes and Real-Lifes', *Listener*, 4 May 1972
Robert Melville, 'Pots and Pans', *New Statesman*, 5 May 1972
Hilton Kramer, 'Painterly Subtleties Fill Work of Scott', *New York Times*, 6 January 1973
Terence Flanagan, 'The Drawings of William Scott', *Arts in Ireland*, vol.1, no.3, 1973
Hilton Kramer, 'Art: Seeing an Emotion's Shape', *New York Times*, 11 January 1975
Brian Fallon, Obituary of William Scott, *Irish Times*, 30 December 1989
William Feaver, Obituary of William Scott, *Observer*, 31 December 1989
Norbert Lynton, Obituary of William Scott, *The Independent*, 2 January 1990
Alan Bowness (with Adrian Heath), Obituary of William Scott, *Guardian*, 5 January 1990
Patrick Heron, Obituary of William Scott, *Art Monthly*, February 1990
Patrick Heron, 'William Scott', *Modern Painters*, vol.2, no.4, Winter 1990–91
Alfred Janes, 'William Scott: a life study', *Independent*, 12 April 1997
Sarah Whitfield and Lucy Inglis, 'William Scott's War', *Burlington Magazine*, April 2008
David Anfam, 'The Planet on the Table', *William Scott*, McCaffrey Fine Art, New York, February–April 2010

GENERAL

Lawrence Alloway, *Nine Abstract Artists: Their Work and Theory*, London 1954
Patrick Heron, *The Changing Forms of Art*, London 1955
Bryan Robertson, John Russell, and Lord Snowdon, *Private View*, London 1965
Mel Gooding, *Patrick Heron*, London 1994
Derek Pope (ed.), *A Celebration of Bath Academy of Art at Corsham*, Corsham 1997

Margaret Garlake, *New Art, New World: British Art in Postwar Society*, London and New Haven 1998
James Hall, *The Battle for Realism: Figurative Art in Britain during the Cold War 1945–1960*, New Haven and London 2001
Blast to Freeze: British Art in the 20th Century, exh. cat., Kunstmuseum Wolfsburg 2002
Adrian Lewis, *Roger Hilton*, Aldershot 2003
Jane Rye, *Adrian Heath*, London 2012

ACKNOWLEDGEMENTS

This book comes out of the research done for the *William Scott Catalogue Raisonné of Oil Paintings*, a project generously sponsored by the artist's sons Robert and James. Their commitment to their father's work, their own knowledge of his life and his art, and their invaluable input at every stage made the whole enterprise possible. Over the six years it took to complete the project, I had the constant help and support of Dr Lucy Inglis, whose impressive research at every level greatly helped build the structure on which the catalogue raisonné is based. My thanks to her cannot be expressed too fully. Many others were involved over the years, including Hester Russell Grant, Charlie Whitehead and most recently Purwita Susanto, who was particularly involved in the latter and particularly demanding stages leading up to publication of the catalogue raisonné in 2013. Many times, and in many ways, Lisa Scott helped smooth the way forward, for which I am grateful. I would also like to thank Sir Alan Bowness, author of the first major book on Scott, who gave up much of his time to talk about the artist and to share the files he has kept over the years. Lastly, but perhaps most crucially, I must thank Herman Lelie, who got me involved with William Scott in the first place.

COPYRIGHT CREDITS

PHOTO CREDITS

Altnagelvin Hospital, Londonderry, Northern Ireland fig.50
Bernard Jacobson Gallery fig.13
André Emmerich Gallery fig.23
Carla Lemos Ferreira fig.42
Columbia University fig.45
Gallery Moos fig.55
Hazlitt Holland-Hibbert fig.37
Trustees of The Higgins Art Gallery & Museum, Bedford fig.33
Colin Mills figs. 1, 2, 3, 5, 6, 7, 8, 9, 10, 11, 12, 14, 15, 16, 17, 18, 19, 22, 26, 28, 32, 36, 44, 52, 53, 54, 58, 59, 60
Brian Rutledge figs.31, 46, 48
© 2012. Albright-Knox Art Gallery/ Art Resource, NY/Scala, Florence figs.43, 56
Mischa Scott figs.21, 38, 57
Robert Scott fig.51
Lee Stalsworth figs.24, 40
Tate Photography figs. 4, 20, 25, 27, 29, 30, 34, 35, 49
Tate Photography/Samuel Drake frontispiece
John Webb, Brompton Studio fig.39
G Winters fig.19

INDEX